QuEST

Vol 2

Spiritual Thoughts and Talk Starters

By

Jeff Cheney

QuEST

What is a QUEST?

Several years ago, as our children were young, they were assigned to give talks and spiritual thoughts. As we live in a small Branch of The Church of Jesus Christ of Latter-day Saints, this opportunity came very often.

One day our oldest daughter asked my wife what she needed to put into her talk. What she was looking for was the minimum. What did she have to put in to consider it a complete talk.

My wife is one of the brightest people on the face of the earth; she was also an elementary teacher and a seminary teacher at that time, so she was not going to be fooled into giving an easy answer to my daughter. The answer that she gave, however, became a standard in our home and is the basis for this book. She told her that for her talk, and every talk, she needed to have a quote, an experience or story, a scripture and a testimony. We shortened this into Quest.

QU ote

E xperience

S cripture

T estimony

Many years later, we had six missionaries serving from our Branch in many parts of the world. These six included our youngest son, Drew. Because this was such a special time for our Branch, I wanted to do something special for these missionaries. I decided that while they were serving, I would send them a spiritual thought every week in the form of a Quest. As a result, these quests were started.

I have continued to create them and send them, every week, to my nieces and nephews who are serving missions, as well as any missionaries serving from our Branch.

I just thought I would share them with you. I hope they are useful for those times when you need a spiritual thought or a start for a talk.

~Jeff Cheney

Table of Contents

Quest #31
Humility

Quote:

"The first test of a truly great man is his humility. I do not mean, by humility, doubt of his own power…[but really] great men… have a curious… feeling that… greatness is not in them, but through them… and they see something Divine… in every other man, and are endlessly, foolishly, incredibly merciful."

~John Ruskin

Experience:

"Recently during a special women's conference, a speaker told about how he'd been quite successful in land development and how everything he'd touched had turned to gold. He'd also tried to live a faithful life and had been a very active servant in the gospel. Then he'd been called as a mission president. He had apparently been a very effective mission president and had subsequently returned to his home state. Throughout his life he'd experienced one success after another—he was a recognized leader in his community, had built a prosperous business. Being called as a mission president had sort of cemented in his mind that he'd "made it"—that he was an all-around success.

When he returned from his mission, a combination of changing interest rates and other business factors caused his once-prosperous business to plummet. In fact, he'd lost nearly everything. Telling the story, this man said, "I realized that I'd become quite boastful—that while I felt I had a testimony of Jesus Christ, in my mind I had brought about all of these wonderful things through my hard work, intelligence, and so forth. But when hard times hit, I began to realize how offensive I must have been to others and to my Heavenly Father to assume that I had brought all of these good things on my own. I felt like I'd lived a life of arrogance and boasting."

~Elder Marvin J. Ashton   April 1990

Scripture:

"Blessed are they who humble themselves without being compelled to be humble."

~Alma 32:16

Testimony:

"We must yield "to the enticings of the Holy Spirit," put off the prideful "natural man," become "a saint through the atonement of Christ the Lord," and become "as a child, submissive, meek, humble."

That we may do so and go on to fulfill our divine destiny is my fervent prayer in the name of Jesus Christ, amen."

~President Ezra Taft Benson   April 1989

Quest #32
Serving Without Expectations

Quote:

"Not all of us are going to be like Moroni, catching the acclaim of our colleagues all day every day. Most of us will be quiet, relatively unknown folks who come and go and do our work without fanfare. To those of you who may find that [thought] lonely or frightening or just unspectacular, I say, you are "no less serviceable" than the most spectacular of your associates. You, too, are part of God's army."
~*President Howard W. Hunter   April 1992*

Experience:

"Oliver Granger is the kind of quiet, supportive individual in the latter days that the Lord remembered in section 117 of the Doctrine and Covenants. Oliver's name may be unfamiliar to many, so I will take the liberty to acquaint you with this early stalwart.

Oliver Granger was eleven years older than Joseph Smith and, like the Prophet, was from upstate New York. Because of severe cold and exposure when he was thirty-three years old, Oliver lost much of his eyesight. Notwithstanding his limited vision, he served three full-time missions. He also worked on the Kirtland Temple and served on the Kirtland high council.

When most of the Saints were driven from Kirtland, Ohio, the Church left some debts unsatisfied. Oliver was appointed to represent Joseph Smith and the First Presidency by returning to Kirtland to settle the Church's business. Of this task, the Doctrine and Covenants records: "Therefore, let him contend earnestly for the redemption of the First Presidency of my Church, saith the Lord." (D&C 117:13.)

He performed this assignment with such satisfaction to the creditors involved that one of them wrote: "Oliver Granger's management in the arrangement of the unfinished business of people that have moved to the Far West, in redeeming their pledges and thereby sustaining their integrity, has been truly praiseworthy, and has entitled him to my highest esteem, and every grateful recollection." (Horace Kingsbury, as cited in Joseph Smith, History of the Church, 3:174.)

During Oliver's time in Kirtland, some people, including disaffected members of the Church, were endeavoring to discredit the First Presidency and bring their integrity into question by spreading false accusations. Oliver Granger, in very deed, "redeemed the First Presidency" through his faithful service. ... The Lord said of Oliver Granger:

"His name shall be had in sacred remembrance from generation to generation, forever and ever." (D&C 117:12.) "I will lift up my servant Oliver, and beget for him a great name on the earth, and among my people, because of the integrity of his soul." (History of the Church, 3:350.)

When he died in 1841, even though there were but few Saints remaining in the Kirtland area and even fewer friends of the Saints, Oliver Granger's funeral was attended by a vast concourse of people from neighboring towns."
~President Howard W. Hunter   April 1992

Scripture:
"Behold, I say unto you that because I said unto you that I had spent my days in your service, I do not desire to boast, for I have only been in the service of God. And behold, I tell you these things that ye may learn wisdom; that ye may learn that when ye are in the service of your fellow beings ye are only in the service of your God."
~Mosiah 2:16–17

Testimony:
"If you feel that much of what you do does not make you very famous, take heart. Most of the best people who ever lived weren't very famous, either. Serve and grow, faithfully and quietly. Be on guard regarding the praise of men. Jesus said in the Sermon on the Mount:

"Take heed that ye do not your alms before men, to be seen of them: otherwise ye have no reward of your Father which is in heaven.

"Therefore when thou doest thine alms, do not sound a trumpet before thee, as the hypocrites do in the synagogues and in the streets, that they may have glory of men. Verily I say unto you, They have their reward.

"But when thou doest alms, let not thy left hand know what thy right hand doeth:

"That thine alms may be in secret: and thy Father which seeth in secret himself shall reward thee openly." (Matt. 6:1–4.)

May our Father in Heaven so reward you always."
~President Howard W. Hunter   April 1992

Quest #33
Work

Quote:
"Happy is the man who has work he loves to do. ... Happy is the man who loves the work he has to do"
~Anonymous

Experience:
"Lately I have been thinking of a time in my life when the weight of worry and concern over an uncertain future seemed ever present. I was 11 years old and living with my family in the attic of a farmhouse near Frankfurt, Germany. We were refugees for the second time in a period of only a few years, and we were struggling to establish ourselves in a new place far away from our previous home. I could say that we were poor, but that would be an understatement. We all slept in one room that was so tiny there was scarcely space to walk around the beds. In the other small room, we had a few pieces of modest furniture and a stove that Mother used to cook meals on. To get from one room to the other, we had to pass through a storage area where the farmer kept his equipment and tools, along with assorted meats and sausages hanging from the rafters. The aroma always made me very hungry. We had no bathroom, but we did have an outhouse—down the stairs and some 50 feet (15 m) away, though it seemed much farther during wintertime.

Because I was a refugee and because of my East German accent, other children often made fun of me and called me names that deeply hurt. Of all the times of my youth, I believe this may have been the most discouraging.

Now, decades later, I can look back on those days through the softening filter of experience. Even though I still remember the hurt and despair, I can see now what I was unable to see then: this was a period of great personal growth. During this time, our family bonded together. I watched and learned from my parents. I admired their determination and optimism. From them I learned that adversity, when confronted with faith, courage, and tenacity, could be overcome.

To this day, I am deeply impressed by the way my family worked after having lost everything following World War II! I remember my father—a civil servant by education and experience—taking on several difficult jobs, among which were coal miner, uranium miner, mechanic, and truck driver. He left early in the morning and often returned late at night in order to support our family. My mother started a laundry and worked countless hours doing menial labor. She enlisted my sister and me in her business. With my bike I became the pickup and delivery service. It felt good to be able to help the family in a small way, and though I did not know it at the time, the physical labor turned out to be a blessing to my health as well.

It wasn't easy, but the work kept us from dwelling too much on the difficulties of our circumstances. Although our situation didn't change overnight, it did change."

~President Dieter F. Uchtdorf   October 2009

Scripture:

"Thou shalt not idle away thy time, neither shalt thou bury thy talent"
~D&C 60:13

Testimony:

"I pray that during the coming months and years we can fill our hours and days with righteous work. I pray that we will seek to learn and improve our minds and hearts by drinking deeply from the pure fountains of truth. I leave you my love and blessings in the name of Jesus Christ, amen."

~President Dieter F. Uchtdorf   October 2009

Quest #34
Christlike Character

Quote:

"Man's chief concern in life should not be the acquiring of gold, or of fame, or of material possessions. It should not be the development of physical prowess, nor of intellectual strength, but his aim, the highest in life, should be the development of a Christ-like character."
~President David O. McKay

Experience:

"A few years ago, my wife and I stood at the trailhead of Japan's highest mountain, Mount Fuji. As we began our ascent we looked up to the far-distant summit and wondered if we could get there.

As we progressed, fatigue, sore muscles, and the effects of altitude set in. Mentally, it became important for us to focus on just the next step. We would say, "I may not soon make it to the top, but I can do this next step right now." Over time the daunting task ultimately became achievable—step by step.

The first step on this path to becoming like Jesus Christ is to have the desire to do so. Understanding the admonition to be like Him is good, but that understanding needs to be coupled with a yearning to transform ourselves, one step at a time, beyond the natural man.'
~ Elder Scott D. Whiting   October 2020

Scripture:

"Therefore, what manner of men ought ye to be? Verily I say unto you, even as I am."
~3 Nephi 27: 27

Testimony:

"I am convinced that the Master was not merely thinking relatively when he said, 'Be ye therefore perfect, even as your Father which is in heaven is perfect.' [Matthew 5:48.] ... Would you suppose the Savior was suggesting a goal that was not possible of attainment and thus mock us in our efforts to live to attain that perfectness? It is impossible for us here in mortality to come to that state of perfection of which the Master spoke, but in this life we lay the foundation on which we will build in eternity; therefore, we must make sure that our foundation is laid on truth, righteousness and faith. In order for us to reach that goal we must keep God's commandments and be true to the end of our lives here, and then beyond the grave continue in righteousness and knowledge until we become as our Father in Heaven. ...

"... [The Apostle Paul] pointed to the course by which perfection comes. Speaking of Jesus, he said, 'Though he were a Son, yet learned he obedience by the things which he suffered; and being made perfect, he became the author of eternal salvation unto all them that obey him.' (Hebrews 5:8–9.) ...

"... Let then no day pass but that we learn from the great lesson book of [Christ's] life his way to a perfect life and walk therein to our eternal goal."

~President Harold B. Lee   Decisions for Successful Living (1973), 40-41, 44.

Quest #35
Christlike Love

Quote:

"Our desire to serve others is magnified by our gratitude for what the Savior has done for us. That is why our hearts swell when we hear the words sung "Because I have been given much, I too must give."
~*President Henry B. Eyring   April 2016*

Experience:

"May I share with you an experience that has impacted and changed my life. Ted and Sharon, Cooper's parents, who are here today, have given me permission to share what happened to their family more than nine years ago. I will tell the experience from the perspective of Ted, Cooper's father:"

"August 21, 2008, was the first day of school, and Cooper's three older brothers, Ivan, Garrett, and Logan, were all at the bus stop waiting to board buses. Cooper, who was four years old, was on his bike; my wife, Sharon, had walked.

My wife was across the street and motioned to Cooper to cross. At the same time, a car very slowly made a left turn and rolled over Cooper. I received a phone call from a neighbor telling me Cooper had been hit by a car. I quickly drove down to the bus stop to see him. Cooper was lying on the grass, struggling to breathe, but had no visible injuries.

I knelt down by Cooper and said encouraging things like "It's going to be OK. Hang on." At that moment my high priests group leader, Nathan, appeared with his wife. She suggested we give Cooper a priesthood blessing. We laid our hands on Cooper's head. I can't remember what I said in the blessing, but I clearly remember the presence of others around us, and it was at that moment I knew Cooper was going to pass away.

Cooper was flown by helicopter to the hospital but did, in fact, pass away. I felt Heavenly Father was telling me that my earthly stewardship had ended and that Cooper was now in His care.

We were able to spend some time with Cooper at the hospital. The workers there prepared him so we could hold him and say our goodbyes and allowed us to spend as much time with him, holding him, as we desired.

On the way home, my grief-stricken wife and I looked at each other and started talking about the boy who was driving the car. We didn't know him, even though he lived just one street over and was within our ward boundaries.

The next day was very difficult for us as we were all completely overwhelmed with grief. I fell to my knees and prayed the most sincere prayer I had ever offered. I asked Heavenly Father in the name of my Savior to take away my overwhelming grief. He did so.

Later that day one of the counselors in our stake presidency arranged for us to meet with the young man—the driver of the car—and his parents at the counselor's home. Sharon and I waited for the boy and his parents to arrive. When the door opened, we met them for the first time. My bishop whispered in my ear, "Go to him." Sharon and I embraced him in a big group hug. We wept together for what seemed to be a long time. We told him we knew that what had happened was the definition of an accident.

It was miraculous to Sharon and me, both that we felt the way we did and that we still do. By God's grace, we were able to take the big path, the obvious path, the only path, and love this good young man.

We have become very close to him and his family over the years. He has shared his most precious milestone moments with us. We even went to the temple with him as he prepared for his mission.'

~ By Elder Jose L. Alonso   October 2017

Scripture:

"Thou shalt love the Lord thy God with all thy heart, and with all thy soul, and with all thy mind.

"This is the first and great commandment.

"And the second is like unto it, Thou shalt love thy neighbour as thyself."

~Matthew 22: 37-39

Testimony:

"I bear my witness that God the Father lives and wants you to come home to Him. This is the true Church of the Lord Jesus Christ. He knows you; He loves you; He watches over you. He atoned for your sins and mine and the sins of all of Heavenly Father's children. Following Him in your life and in your service to others is the only way to eternal life.

I so testify and leave you my blessing and my love. In the sacred name of Jesus Christ, amen."

~President Henry B. Eyring   October 2017

Quest #36
Healing Atonement

Quote:

Master, with anguish of spirit
I bow in my grief today.
The depths of my sad heart are troubled.
Oh, waken and save, I pray!
Torrents of sin and of anguish
Sweep o'er my sinking soul,
And I perish! I perish! dear Master.
Oh, hasten and take control!
~ *Mary Ann Baker   Master the Tempest is Raging   (Hymns #105)*

Experience:

"Corrie ten Boom, a devout Dutch Christian woman, found such healing despite having been interned in concentration camps during World War II. She suffered greatly, but unlike her beloved sister Betsie, who perished in one of the camps, Corrie survived.

After the war she often spoke publicly of her experiences and of healing and forgiveness. On one occasion a former Nazi guard who had been part of Corrie's own grievous confinement in Ravensbrück, Germany, approached her, rejoicing at her message of Christ's forgiveness and love.

"'How grateful I am for your message, Fraulein,' he said. 'To think that, as you say, He has washed my sins away!'

"His hand was thrust out to shake mine," Corrie recalled. "And I, who had preached so often ... the need to forgive, kept my hand at my side.

"Even as the angry, vengeful thoughts boiled through me, I saw the sin of them. ... Lord Jesus, I prayed, forgive me and help me to forgive him.

"I tried to smile, [and] I struggled to raise my hand. I could not. I felt nothing, not the slightest spark of warmth or charity. And so again I breathed a silent prayer. Jesus, I cannot forgive him. Give me Your forgiveness.

"As I took his hand the most incredible thing happened. From my shoulder along my arm and through my hand a current seemed to pass from me to him, while into my heart sprang a love for this stranger that almost overwhelmed me.

"And so I discovered that it is not on our forgiveness any more than on our goodness that the world's healing hinges, but on His. When He tells us to love our enemies, He gives, along with the command, the love itself."

Corrie ten Boom was made whole.'
~*Elder Timothy J. Dyches of the Seventy*   *October 2013*

Scripture:

"Come unto me, all ye that labour and are heavy laden, and I will give you rest.

Take my yoke upon you, and learn of me; for I am meek and lowly in heart : and ye shall find rest unto your souls.

For my yoke is easy, and my burden is light."
~*Matthew 11:28–30*

Testimony:

"I know these things to be true. Our Savior's Atonement does more than assure us of immortality by a universal resurrection and give us the opportunity to be cleansed from sin by repentance and baptism. His Atonement also provides the opportunity to call upon Him who has experienced all of our mortal infirmities to give us the strength to bear the burdens of mortality. He knows of our anguish, and He is there for us. Like the good Samaritan, when He finds us wounded at the wayside, He will bind up our wounds and care for us (see Luke 10:34). The healing and strengthening power of Jesus Christ and His Atonement is for all of us who will ask. I testify of that as I also testify of our Savior, who makes it all possible.

One day all of these mortal burdens will pass away and there will be no more pain (see Revelation 21:4). I pray that we will all understand the hope and strength of our Savior's Atonement: the assurance of immortality, the opportunity for eternal life, and the sustaining strength we can receive if only we will ask, in the name of Jesus Christ, amen."
~*Elder Dallin H. Oaks   October 2015*

Quest #37
The Power of the Book of Mormon

Quote:

"The Book of Mormon teaches us truth [and] bears testimony of Christ. ... But there is something more. There is a power in the book which will begin to flow into your lives the moment you begin a serious study of the book. You will find greater power to resist temptation. ... You will find the power to stay on the strait and narrow path."

~President Ezra Taft Benson   October 1986

Experience:

"In my case the Book of Mormon became the keystone of my testimony over a period of years and through a number of experiences. One powerful experience in forming my testimony occurred while I was a young missionary serving in my first area: Kumamoto, Japan. My companion and I were house-to-house proselyting. I met a grandmother who kindly invited us into the entry of her home, which is called a *genkan* in Japanese. She offered us a cold drink on a hot day. I had not been in Japan very long, and I had recently completed reading the Book of Mormon and had been praying to know with certainty that it was true. Because of my newness to Japan, I didn't speak Japanese very well. In fact, I don't think this woman understood much of what I was saying. I began teaching her about the Book of Mormon, describing how Joseph Smith received from an angel an ancient record engraved on plates and how he translated them by the power of God.

As I offered her my testimony that the Book of Mormon is the word of God and another testament of Jesus Christ, I received the strongest impression, accompanied by a warm feeling of comfort and serenity inside my chest, which the scriptures describe as "your bosom [burning] within you."[4] This feeling reaffirmed to me in a powerful way that the Book of Mormon truly is the word of God. At that time my feelings were so strong that tears came to my eyes as I talked to this Japanese grandmother. I have never forgotten the special feeling of that day.'

~Elder Gary E. Stevenson   October 2016

Scripture:

"Feast upon the words of Christ; for behold, the words of Christ will tell you all things what ye should do"

~2 Nephi 32:3

Testimony:

"Now, I did not sail with the brother of Jared in crossing an ocean, settling in a new world. I did not hear King Benjamin speak his angelically delivered sermon. I did not proselyte with Alma and Amulek nor witness the fiery death of innocent believers. I was not among the Nephite crowd who touched the wounds of the resurrected Lord, nor did I weep with Mormon and Moroni over the destruction of an entire civilization. But my testimony of this record and the peace it brings to the human heart is as binding and unequivocal as was theirs. Like them, "[I] give [my name] unto the world, to witness unto the world that which [I] *have seen.*" And like them, "[I] lie not, God bearing witness of it."

I ask that my testimony of the Book of Mormon and all that it implies, given today under my own oath and office, be recorded by men on earth and angels in heaven. I hope I have a few years left in my "last days," but whether I do or do not, I want it absolutely clear when I stand before the judgment bar of God that I declared to the world, in the most straightforward language I could summon, that the Book of Mormon is true, that it came forth the way Joseph said it came forth and was given to bring happiness and hope to the faithful in the travail of the latter days."

~Elder Jeffrey R. Holland   October 2009

Quest #38
Prophets

Quote:

"The obligation that we make when we raise our hands ... is a most sacred one. It does not mean that we will go quietly on our way and be willing that the prophet of the Lord shall direct this work, but it means ... that we will stand behind him; we will pray for him; we will defend his good name, and we will strive to carry out his instructions as the Lord shall direct."

~Elder George Albert Smith (26 years before he became President of the Church)

Experience:

"How do we really sustain a prophet? Long before he became President of the Church, President Joseph F. Smith explained, "It is an important duty resting upon the Saints who ... sustain the authorities of the Church, to do so not only by the lifting of the hand, the mere form, but in *deed* and in truth."

Well do I remember my most unique "deed" to sustain a prophet. As a medical doctor and cardiac surgeon, I had the responsibility of performing open-heart surgery on President Spencer W. Kimball in 1972, when he was Acting President of the Quorum of the Twelve Apostles. He needed a very complex operation. But I had no experience doing such a procedure on a 77-year-old patient in heart failure. I did not recommend the operation and so informed President Kimball and the First Presidency. But, in faith, President Kimball chose to have the operation, only because it was advised by the First Presidency. That shows how he sustained his leaders! And his decision made me tremble!

Thanks to the Lord, the operation was a success. When President Kimball's heart resumed beating, it did so with great power! At that very moment, I had a clear witness of the Spirit that this man would one day become President of the Church!

You know the outcome. Only 20 months later, President Kimball became President of the Church. And he provided bold and courageous leadership for many years.

Since then we have sustained Presidents Ezra Taft Benson, Howard W. Hunter, Gordon B. Hinckley, and now Thomas S. Monson as Presidents of the Church—prophets in every sense of the word!"
~President Russell M. Nelson   October 2014

Scripture:

" Surely the Lord God will do nothing, but he revealeth his secret unto his servants the prophets."
~Amos 3:7

Testimony:

"I testify of this reaching, rescuing, merciful Jesus, that this is His redeeming Church based on His redeeming love, and that, as those in the Book of Mormon declared, "there came prophets among the people, who were sent from the Lord [to speak it]. ... [Yea,] there came prophets in the land again." I testify that President Gordon B. Hinckley is in every way, from head to toe, such a prophet, one whose life and voice we cherish and for whom we have prayed so much. He will now conclude this semiannual gathering. For such a blessing—and *all* these blessings and so many more— I give personal thanks at general conference time, in the name of Jesus Christ, amen."
~Elder Jeffrey R. Holland   October 2006

Quest #39
Strengthen Each Other

Quote:

"All of us have far too much to do to waste our time and energies in criticism, faultfinding, or the abuse of others. The Lord has commanded us to refrained from these things. And then follows the marvelous promise that He will bless us and deliver us forever."
~President Gordon B. Hinckley   (Stand a Little Taller)

Experience:

"Some years ago I was called, with my wife, Jacqui, to preside over the Washington Spokane Mission. We arrived in the mission field with a mix of fear and excitement at the responsibility of working with so many remarkable young missionaries. They came from many different backgrounds and quickly became like our own sons and daughters.

Although most were doing wonderfully well, a few were struggling with the high expectations of their calling. I remember one missionary telling me, "President, I just don't like people." Several told me they lacked the desire to follow the rather strict missionary rules. I worried and wondered what we could do to change the hearts of those few missionaries who had not yet learned the joy of being obedient.

One day while driving through the beautiful rolling wheat fields on the Washington-Idaho border, I was listening to a recording of the New Testament. As I listened to the familiar account of the rich young man coming to the Savior to ask what he might do to have eternal life, I received an unexpected but profound personal revelation that is now a sacred memory.

After hearing Jesus recite the commandments and the young man reply that he had observed all these since his youth, I listened for the Savior's gentle correction: "One thing thou lackest: ... sell whatsoever thou hast, and ... come, ... follow me." But to my astonishment, I instead heard six words before that part of the verse that I seemed never to have heard or read before. It was as if they had been added to the scriptures. I marveled at the inspired understanding which then unfolded.

What were these six words that had such a profound effect? Listen to see if you can recognize these seemingly ordinary words, not found in the other Gospel accounts but found only in the Gospel of Mark:

"There came one running ... and asked him, Good Master, what shall I do that I may inherit eternal life?

"And Jesus said unto him, ...

"Thou knowest the commandments, Do not commit adultery, Do not kill, Do not steal, Do not bear false witness, Defraud not, Honour thy father and mother.

"And he answered ... , Master, all these have I observed from my youth.

"*Then Jesus beholding him loved him,* and said unto him, One thing thou lackest: go thy way, sell whatsoever thou hast, and give to the poor, and thou shalt have treasure in heaven: and come, take up the cross, and follow me."

"Then Jesus beholding him loved him."

As I heard these words, a vivid image filled my mind of our Lord pausing and *beholding* this young man. *Beholding*—as in looking deeply and penetratingly into his soul, recognizing his goodness and also his potential, as well as discerning his greatest need.

Then the simple words—Jesus *loved him.* He felt an overwhelming love and compassion for this good young man, and *because* of this love and *with* this love, Jesus asked even more of him. I pictured what it must have felt like for this young man to be enveloped by such love even while being asked to do something so supremely hard as selling all he owned and giving it to the poor.

In that moment, I knew It was not just the hearts of some of our missionaries that needed changing. It was my heart as well. The question no longer was "How does a frustrated mission president get a struggling missionary to behave better?" Instead, the question was "How can I be filled with Christlike love so a missionary can feel the love of God through me and desire to change?" How can I *behold* him or her in the same way the Lord beheld the rich young man, seeing them for who they really are and who they can become, rather than just for what they are doing or not doing? How can I be more like the Savior?   *"Then Jesus beholding him loved him."*

From that time forward, as I sat knee to knee with a young missionary struggling with some aspect of obedience, within my heart I now saw a faithful young man or young woman who had acted on the desire to come on a mission. Then I was able to say with all the feeling like that of a tender parent: "Elder or Sister, if I didn't love you, I wouldn't care what happens on your mission. But I do love you, and because I love you, I care about who you become. So I invite you to change those things that are hard for you and become who the Lord wants you to be."
~Elder S. Mark Palmer   April 2017

Scripture:
"Therefore, strengthen your brethren in all your conversation, in all your prayers, in all your exhortations, and in all your doings.

    And behold, and lo, I am with you to bless you and deliver you forever. Amen."
~Doctrine and Covenants 108:7-8

Testimony:
"Let us serve others humbly—with energy, gratitude, and honor. Even though our acts of service may seem lowly, modest, or of little value, those who reach out in kindness and compassion to others will one day know the value of their service by the eternal and blessed grace of Almighty God.

    My dear brethren, dear friends, may we meditate upon, understand, and live this paramount lesson of Church leadership and priesthood governance: "He that is greatest among you shall be your servant." This is my prayer and blessing in the sacred name of our Master, our Redeemer, in the name of Jesus Christ, amen."
~President Dieter F. Uchtdorf   April 2017

Quest #40
Be Wise

Quote:

Sweet is the peace the gospel brings
To seeking minds and true.
With light refulgent on its wings,
It clears the human view.
  Its laws and precepts are divine
And show a Father's care.
Transcendent love and mercy shine
In each injunction there.
  Faithless tradition flees its pow'r,
And unbelief gives way.
The gloomy clouds, which used to low'r,
Submit to reason's sway.

~Mary Ann Morton Durham   *Sweet Is the Peace the Gospel Brings*
(Hymns #14)

Experience:

"Brothers and sisters, while I was studying the Book of Mormon recently, one of the teachings of the prophet Jacob caught my attention. As you remember, Jacob was one of Father Lehi's two sons born in the wilderness after the family left Jerusalem. He was an eyewitness to miracles, and he also watched as his family was torn apart by disobedience and rebellion. Jacob knew and loved Laman and Lemuel as he knew and loved Nephi, and the dissension between them was intimate and personal. As far as Jacob was concerned, it wasn't about ideology, philosophy, or even theology. It was about family.

The tender anguish of Jacob's soul is evident as he expresses grave concern that his people will "reject the words of the prophets" concerning Christ and "deny ... the power of God, and the gift of the Holy Ghost, ... and make a mock of the great plan of redemption" (Jacob 6:8).

And then, just before he bids farewell, he speaks eight simple words that are the basic text of my message this morning. Jacob's plea was "O be wise; what can I say more?" (Jacob 6:12).

Those of you who are parents and grandparents have a sense of what Jacob must have been feeling at the time. He loved his people, partly because they were also his family. He had taught them as clearly as he could and with all the energy of his soul. He warned them in no uncertain terms what would happen if they chose not to "enter in at the strait gate, and continue in the way which is narrow" (Jacob 6:11). He couldn't think of anything else to say to warn, to urge, to inspire, to motivate. And so he, simply and profoundly, said, "O be wise; what can I say more?"
~Elder M. Russell Ballard   October 2006

Scripture:

"O then, my beloved brethren, repent ye, and enter in at the strait gate, and continue in the way which is narrow, until ye shall obtain eternal life.

O be wise; what can I say more?"

~Jacob 6:11-12

Testimony:

"Today is in many ways like Jacob's day. My counsel is like unto his: "Repent, and come with full purpose of heart, and cleave unto God as he cleaveth unto you" (Jacob 6:5). Brothers and sisters, be wise with your families. Be wise in fulfilling your Church callings. Be wise with your time. Be wise in balancing all of your responsibilities. O be wise, my beloved brothers and sisters. What can I say more?

May God bless us with wisdom to love His Son, Jesus Christ, and wisely help accomplish His work. I bear my witness and testimony that He lives. This is His Church. We are about His work. May the peace of the Lord be with us. And may we wisely carry on our responsibilities, I humbly pray, in the name of Jesus Christ, amen."

~Elder M. Russell Ballard   October 2006

Quest #41
Obedience

Quote:

"The happiness of the Latter-day Saints, the peace of the Latter-day Saints, the progress of the Latter-day Saints, the prosperity of the Latter-day Saints, and the eternal salvation and exaltation of this people lie in walking in obedience to the counsels of ... God."

~*President Gordon B. Hinckley*

"Obedience is the first law of heaven."

~*President Joseph F. Smith*

"Stay on the Lord's side of the line."

~*President George Albert Smith*

"The greatest message that one in this position could give to the membership of the Church is to keep the commandments of God, for therein lies the safety of the Church and the safety of the individual. Keep the commandments. There could be nothing that I could say that would be a more powerful or important message today."

~*President Harold B. Lee*

"Happiness is the object and design of our existence; and will be the end thereof, if we pursue the path that leads to it; and this path is virtue, uprightness, faithfulness, holiness, and keeping all the commandments of God."

~*Joseph Smith*

Experience:

"Throughout the years, I have known countless individuals who have been particularly faithful and obedient. I have been blessed and inspired by them. May I share with you an account of two such individuals.

Walter Krause was a steadfast member of the Church who, with his family, lived in what became known as East Germany following the Second World War. Despite the hardships he faced because of the lack of freedom in that area of the world at the time, Brother Krause was a man who loved and served the Lord. He faithfully and conscientiously fulfilled each assignment given to him.

The other man, Johann Denndorfer, a native of Hungary, was converted to the Church in Germany and was baptized there in 1911 at the age of 17. Not too long afterward he returned to Hungary. Following the Second World War, he found himself virtually a prisoner in his native land, in the city of Debrecen. Freedom had also been taken from the people of Hungary.

Brother Walter Krause, who did not know Brother Denndorfer, received the assignment to be his home teacher and to visit him on a regular basis. Brother Krause called his home teaching companion and said to him, "We have received an assignment to visit Brother Johann Denndorfer. Would you be available to go with me this week to see him and give him a gospel message?" And then he added, "Brother Denndorfer lives in Hungary."

His startled companion asked, "When will we leave?"

"Tomorrow," came the reply from Brother Krause.

"When will we return home?" asked the companion.

Brother Krause responded, "Oh, in about a week—if we *get* back."

Away the two home teaching companions went to visit Brother Denndorfer, traveling by train and bus from the northeastern area of Germany to Debrecen, Hungary—a substantial journey. Brother Denndorfer had not had home teachers since before the war. Now, when he saw these servants of the Lord, he was overwhelmed with gratitude that they had come. At first he declined to shake hands with them. Rather, he went to his bedroom and took from a small cabinet a box containing his tithing that he had saved for years. He presented the tithing to his home teachers and said, "Now I am current with the Lord. *Now* I feel worthy to shake the hands of servants of the Lord!" Brother Krause told me later that he had been touched beyond words to think that this faithful brother, who had no contact with the Church for many years, had obediently and consistently taken from his meager earnings 10 percent with which to pay his tithing. He had saved it not knowing when or if he might have the privilege of paying it.

Brother Walter Krause passed away nine years ago at the age of 94. He served faithfully and obediently throughout his life and was an inspiration to me and to all who knew him. When asked to fulfill assignments, he never questioned, he never murmured, and he never made excuses."
~President Thomas S. Monson   April 2013

Scripture:

"And it came to pass that I, Nephi, said unto my father: I will go and do the things which the Lord hath commanded, for I know that the Lord giveth no commandments unto the children of men, save he shall prepare a way for them that they may accomplish the thing which he commandeth them.

~1 Nephi 3:7

Testimony:

"I bear my special witness that our Savior lives. Because He obeyed, "every knee shall bow, and every tongue confess … that he is [our Savior]." May we love Him so deeply and believe Him in faith so completely that we too obey, keep His commandments, and return to live with Him forever in the kingdom of our God is my prayer in the name of Jesus Christ, amen."

~Elder Robert D. Hales   April 2014

Quest #42
Overcoming Adversity

Quote:

"Good timber does not grow with ease,

The stronger wind, the stronger trees.

The further sky, the greater length.

The more the storm, the more the strength.

By sun and cold, by rain and snow,

In trees and men good timbers grow."

~Douglas Malloch

Experience:

"Thomas Giles, a Welsh convert who joined the Church in 1844, also suffered much in his lifetime. He was a miner, and while he was digging coal in the mine, a large piece of coal hit him on the head and inflicted a wound nine inches long. The doctor who examined him said the injured man would not live longer than 24 hours. But then the elders came and administered to him. He was promised that he would get well, and that "even if he would never see again, he would live to do much good in the Church." Brother Giles did indeed live but was blind the rest of his life. Within a month of his injury "he was out traveling through the country attending to his ecclesiastical duties."

In 1856 Brother Giles and his family immigrated to Utah, but before he left his homeland, the Welsh Saints presented him with a harp, which he learned to play skillfully. At Council Bluffs he joined a handcart company and headed west. "Though blind he pulled a handcart from Council Bluffs to Salt Lake City." While crossing the plains his wife and two children died. "His sorrow was great and his heart almost broken, but his faith did not fail him. In the midst of his grief he said as did one of old, 'The Lord giveth, and the Lord taketh away; blessed be the name of the Lord.'" When Brother Giles arrived in Salt Lake City, President Brigham Young, who had heard his story, loaned Brother Giles a valuable harp until his own arrived from Wales. Brother Giles "traveled from settlement to settlement in Utah, ... gladdening the hearts of the people with his sweet music."

~President James E. Faust   October 2004

Scripture:

"Remember, remember that it is upon the rock of our Redeemer, who is Christ, the Son of God, that ye must build your foundation; that when the devil shall send forth his mighty winds, yea, his shafts in the whirlwind,

yea, when all his hail and his mighty storm shall beat upon you, it shall have no power over you to drag you down to the gulf of misery and endless wo, because of the rock upon which ye are built, which is a sure foundation, a foundation whereon if men build they cannot fall."
~Helaman 5:12

Testimony:

"As you do, I promise you that you will see the whirlwinds for what they are—tests, temptations, distractions, or challenges to help you grow. And as you live righteously year after year, I assure you that your experiences will confirm to you again and again that Jesus is the Christ. The spiritual rock under your feet will be solid and secure. You will rejoice that God has placed you here to be a part of the final preparations for Christ's glorious return.

The Savior said, "I will not leave you comfortless: I will come to you." This is His promise to you. I know this promise is real. I know that He lives, in the name of Jesus Christ, amen."
~Elder Neil L. Andersen   April 2014

Quest #43
Brightness of Hope

Quote:

"Despair kills ambition, advances sickness, pollutes the soul, and deadens the heart. Despair can seem like a staircase that leads only and forever downward.

Hope, on the other hand, is like the beam of sunlight rising up and above the horizon of our present circumstances. It pierces the darkness with a brilliant dawn."

~President Dieter F. Uchtdorf   October 2008

Experience:

"I owe much of my happiness in life to a man I never met in mortal life. He was an orphan who became one of my great-grandparents. He left me a priceless heritage of hope. Let me tell you some of the part he played in creating that inheritance for me.

His name was Heinrich Eyring. He was born into great wealth. His father, Edward, had a large estate in Coburg, in what is now Germany. His mother was Viscountess Charlotte Von Blomberg. Her father was the keeper of the lands of the king of Prussia.

Heinrich was Charlotte and Edward's first son. Charlotte died at the age of 31, after the birth of her third child. Edward died soon thereafter, having lost all his property and wealth in a failed investment. He was only 40 years of age. He left three orphaned children.

Heinrich, my great-grandfather, had lost both of his parents and a great worldly inheritance. He was penniless. He recorded in his history that he felt his best hope lay in going to America. Although he had neither family nor friends there, he had a feeling of hope about going to America. He first went to New York City. Later he moved to St. Louis, Missouri.

In St. Louis one of his co-workers was a Latter-day Saint. From him he obtained a copy of a pamphlet written by Elder Parley P. Pratt. He read it and then studied every word he could obtain about the Latter-day Saints. He prayed to know if there really were angels that appeared to men, whether there was a living prophet, and whether he had found a true and revealed religion.

After two months of careful study and prayer, Heinrich had a dream in which he was told he was to be baptized. A man whose name and priesthood I hold in sacred memory, Elder William Brown, was to perform the ordinance. Heinrich was baptized in a pool of rainwater on March 11, 1855, at 7:30 in the morning.

I believe that Heinrich Eyring knew then that what I am teaching you today is true. He knew that the happiness of eternal life comes through family bonds which continue forever. Even when he had so recently found the Lord's plan of happiness, he knew that his hope for eternal joy depended on the free choices of others to follow his example. His hope of eternal happiness depended on people not yet born.

As a part of our family's inheritance of hope, he left a history to his descendants."

~President Henry B. Eyring   April 2014

Scripture:

"For whatsoever things were written aforetime were written for our learning, that we through patience and comfort of the scriptures might have hope."

~Romans 15:4,13

Testimony:

"Brothers and sisters, even after the darkest night, the Savior of the world will lead you to a gradual, sweet, and bright dawn that will assuredly rise within you.

As you walk toward the hope of God's light, you will discover the compassion, love, and goodness of a loving Heavenly Father, "in [whom there] is no darkness at all." Of this I testify in the sacred name of Jesus Christ, amen."

~President Dieter F. Uchtdorf   April 2013

Quest #44
Feed My Sheep

Quote:

"Help me reach a friend in darkness;
Help me guide him through the night.
Help me show thy path to glory
By the Spirit's holy light. ...
Help me find thy lambs who wander;
Help me bring them to thy keep.
Teach me, Lord, to be a shepherd;
Father, help me feed thy sheep.
~Elder Robert D. Hales   April 1997

Experience:

"I grew up in rural Salt Lake County when it was an economic necessity to care for a variety of barnyard animals. My favorite animals were sheep—prompted perhaps by the fact that sheep do not require being milked twice a day, seven days a week.

I wanted our own sons to have the blessing of being shepherds to such farm animals. Our older sons were each provided with a ewe to teach them the responsibility of caring for these sheep and the lambs that would hopefully follow.

Our second son, newly turned six years of age, called me excitedly at my office one cold March morning on the phone and said, "Daddy, guess what? Esther [Esther was his mother ewe]—Esther has just had two baby lambs. Please come home and help me take care of them." I instructed Gordon to watch the lambs carefully and make sure they received the mother's milk and they would be fine. I was interrupted by a second phone call later in the morning with the same little voice on the other end saying, "Daddy, these lambs aren't doing very well. They haven't been able to get milk from the mother, and they are very cold. Please come home."

My response likely reflected some of the distress I felt by being distracted from my busy work schedule. I responded, "Gordon, the lambs will be all right. You just watch them, and when Daddy comes home we will make sure they get mother's milk and everything will be fine." Again, later in the afternoon I received a third, more urgent call. Now the voice on the other end was pleading. "Daddy, you've got to come home now. Those lambs are lying down, and one of them looks very cold." Despite work pressures, I now felt some real concern and tried to reassure the six-year-old owner of the mother sheep by saying, "Gordon, bring the lambs into the house. Rub them with a gunnysack to make them warm. When Daddy comes home in a little while, we will milk the mother, feed the lambs, and they will be fine."

Two hours later I drove into the driveway of our home and was met by a boy with tear-stained eyes, carrying a dead lamb in his arms. His grief was overwhelming. Now I tried to make amends by quickly milking the mother sheep and trying to force the milk from a bottle down the throat of the now weak, surviving lamb. At this point, Gordon walked out of the room and came back with a hopeful look in his eyes. He said, "Daddy, I've prayed that we will be able to save this lamb, and I feel it will be all right." The sad note to this story, brethren, is that within a few minutes the second lamb was dead. Then with a look that I will remember forever, this little six-year-old boy who had lost both of his lambs looked up into his father's face and with tears running down his cheeks said, "Daddy, if you had come home when I first called you, we could have saved them both." ~Richard P. Lindsay *April 1994*

Scripture:

"So when they had dined, Jesus saith to Simon Peter, Simon, son of Jonas, lovest thou me more than these? He saith unto him, Yea, Lord; thou knowest that I love thee. He saith unto him, Feed my lambs.

He saith to him again the second time, Simon, son of Jonas, lovest thou me? He saith unto him, Yea, Lord; thou knowest that I love thee. He saith unto him, Feed my sheep.

He saith unto him the third time, Simon, son of Jonas, lovest thou me? Peter was grieved because he said unto him the third time, Lovest thou me? And he said unto him, Lord, thou knowest all things; thou knowest that I love thee. Jesus saith unto him, Feed my sheep."
~John 21:15-17

Testimony:

"The Good Shepherd willingly gave His life for His sheep, for you and me, yes, for all of us, that we might live eternally with our Father in Heaven. I pray that we will all follow the admonition our Savior Jesus Christ gave to Peter three times: "Feed my lambs. ... Feed my sheep. ... Feed my sheep" (John 21:15–17). In the name of Jesus Christ, amen.
~Elder Ben B. Banks October 1999

Quest #45
Testimony

Quote:

"A testimony is not an exhortation; a testimony is not a sermon (none of you are there to exhort the rest); it is not a travelogue. You are there to bear your own witness. It is amazing what you can say in 60 seconds by way of testimony, or 120, or 240, or whatever time you are given, if you confine yourselves to testimony. We'd like to know how you feel. Do you love the work, really? Are you happy in your work? Do you love the Lord? Are you glad that you are a member of the Church?
~*Spencer W. Kimball*

Experience:

"In 1947 Elder Spencer W. Kimball received a letter from his son Andrew, who was serving a full-time mission. Andrew wrote: "I told one fellow ... that I knew of the truthfulness of what I told him, and said that the Holy Ghost had borne witness of it to me. ... When I thought about it later I was a little concerned that I should do such a thing." Because of his concern he said, "I've carefully avoided bearing my testimony to anyone beyond the point of saying 'I feel, I believe, etc.'"

Elder Kimball wrote back to his son. "I think I know exactly how you felt," he said, "for I went through the same experience in my mission. I wanted to be very honest with myself and with the program and with the Lord. For a time I couched my words carefully to try to build up others without actually committing myself to a positive, unequivocal statement that I knew. I felt a little hesitant about it, too, for when I was in tune and doing my duty I felt the Spirit. I really wanted to say that which I really felt, that I knew, but I was reticent. When I approached a positive declaration, it frightened me and yet when I was wholly in tune and spiritually inspired, I wanted to testify. I thought I was being honest, very honest, but then I decided that I was fooling myself. ...

"Undoubtedly, the day you testified to your investigator that you KNEW it was true, the Lord was trying so hard to reveal this truth to you through the power of the Holy Ghost. While you were in the Spirit and in tune and defending the holy program, you felt it deeply, but after you were 'out of the Spirit' and began to reason with yourself and check yourself and question yourself, you wanted to back out. ...

"I have no question in my mind of your testimony. I am sure that you (like I did) have countless golden threads of testimony all through your being only waiting for the hand of the Master Weaver to assemble and weave them into a tapestry of exquisite and perfect design. Now my son, take my advice and QUENCH NOT THE SPIRIT, but whenever the Spirit whispers, follow its holy promptings. Keep in tune spiritually and listen for the promptings and when you are impressed speak out boldly your impressions. The Lord will magnify your testimony and touch hearts. I hope that you will know that there is no criticism herein, but only attempted helpfulness. ...

"I cannot close my epistle to you without bearing you my testimony. I know that it is true⬛—that Jesus is the Creator and Redeemer; that the Gospel taught by us and our 3,000 missionaries is restored and revealed through the real Prophet, Joseph Smith, and is of God, and I have consecrated the balance of my life to 'preaching the kingdom.' I [have borne] my testimony boldly ... and I reaffirm it again and again. I am sure your testimony is the same except perhaps your golden threads need only to be woven into a complete tapestry which will quickly be accomplished in your missionary work as you turn your heart loose and let it rule your mind.

"May God help you to weave into a beautiful pattern the golden threads of your experience and inspiration and may you with always increasing power continue ... to live and teach the everlasting truth."
~President Spencer W. Kimball   Teachings of Presidents of the Church: Spencer W. Kimball, 69–70

Scripture:

"When Jesus came into the coasts of Cæsarea Philippi, he asked his disciples, saying, Whom do men say that I the Son of man am?

And they said, Some say that thou art John the Baptist: some, Elias; and others, Jeremias, or one of the prophets.

He saith unto them, But whom say ye that I am?

And Simon Peter answered and said, Thou art the Christ, the Son of the living God.

And Jesus answered and said unto him, Blessed art thou, Simon Bar-jona: for flesh and blood hath not revealed it unto thee, but my Father which is in heaven.

And I say also unto thee, That thou art Peter, and upon this rock I will build my church; and the gates of hell shall not prevail against it."
~Matthew 16:13-18

Testimony:

"I have met many people who have questioned my testimony. They have said, "Mr. Grant, you cannot know these things." But I am ready and willing to bear testimony that I do know them, and I know them as well as I know light from darkness, warmth from cold. I know after supplicating the Lord I have received answers to my prayers. Therefore, I have a knowledge of these things, and I know them as well as I know that I love my family and my friends. This knowledge has come to me in such a way that I am ready and willing to bear testimony to all the world, and I know that I will have to face the testimony that I bear. I would not be true to myself if I did not, when occasion offered, bear testimony of the things that I do know."

~Heber J. Grant

Quest #46
Revelation

Quote:
"I beseech you, my friends, I beseech you, my brethren and sisters, one and all, to so live that the light of the holy spirit of God may be your constant companion, enlightening your mind, quickening your understanding, inspiring within you a desire to labor with all the power, with all the ability that God has given you for the accomplishment of His purposes."

"Seek the Lord and He will be with you. If we fail to seek the Lord there is no security for any of us. No man or woman who seeks God's Spirit and follows its promptings can fail."

~President Heber J. Grant   Teachings of Presidents of the Church: Heber J. Grant, 182-183

Experience:
"I have a believing heart that started with a simple testimony that came when I was a child—I think maybe I was around ten or eleven years of age. I was with my father out on a farm away from our home, trying to spend the day busying myself until my father was ready to go home. Over the fence from our place were some tumbledown sheds that would attract a curious boy, and I was adventurous. I started to climb through the fence, and I heard a voice as clearly as you are hearing mine, calling me by name and saying, 'Don't go over there!' I turned to look at my father to see if he were talking to me, but he was way up at the other end of the field. There was no person in sight. I realized then, as a child, that there were persons beyond my sight, for I had definitely heard a voice. Since then, when I hear or read stories of the Prophet Joseph Smith, I too have known what it means to hear a voice, because I've had the experience."

~President Harold B. Lee   Stand Ye in Holy Places (1974), 139

Scripture:
Yea, behold, I will tell you in your mind and in your heart, by the Holy Ghost, which shall come upon you and which shall dwell in your heart.

Now, behold, this is the spirit of revelation; behold, this is the spirit by which Moses brought the children of Israel through the Red Sea on dry ground.

~Doctrine and Covenants 8: 2-3

Testimony:

"As you appropriately seek for and apply unto the spirit of revelation, I promise you will "walk in the light of the Lord" (Isaiah 2:5; 2 Nephi 12:5). Sometimes the spirit of revelation will operate immediately and intensely, other times subtly and gradually, and often so delicately you may not even consciously recognize it. But regardless of the pattern whereby this blessing is received, the light it provides will illuminate and enlarge your soul, enlighten your understanding (see Alma 5:7; 32:28), and direct and protect you and your family.

I declare my apostolic witness that the Father and the Son live. The spirit of revelation is real—and can and does function in our individual lives and in The Church of Jesus Christ of Latter-day Saints. I testify of these truths in the sacred name of the Lord Jesus Christ, amen."

~Elder David A. Bednar April 2011

Quest #47
Follow the Prophet

Quote:
"We must have in mind ... that only the President of the Church, the Presiding High Priest, ... has the right to receive revelations for the Church, either new or amendatory, or to give authoritative interpretations of scriptures that shall be binding on the Church. ... He is God's sole mouthpiece on earth for the Church of Jesus Christ of Latter-day Saints, the only true Church. He alone may declare the mind and will of God to his people. No officer of any other Church in the world has this high right and lofty prerogative."
~President J. Reuben Clark Jr.   July 1954

"It is no small thing, my brothers and sisters, to have a prophet of God in our midst. Great and wonderful are the blessings that come into our lives as we listen to the word of the Lord given to us through him."
~Elder M. Russell Ballard_   April 2001

Experience:
Harold B. Lee became the eleventh President of the Church at the passing of President Joseph Fielding Smith in July 1972. Soon thereafter, President Lee visited a room in the Salt Lake Temple where portraits of his ten predecessors were hung.

"There, in prayerful meditation," he recalled, "I looked upon the paintings of those men of God—true, pure men, God's noblemen—who had preceded me in a similar calling." He contemplated the character and achievements of each of the prophets of this last dispensation and finally came to the last portrait. "President Joseph Fielding Smith was there with his smiling face, my beloved prophet-leader who made no compromise with truth. ... He seemed in that brief moment to be passing to me, as it were, a sceptre of righteousness as though to say to me, 'Go thou and do likewise.' ...."
~President Harold B. Lee

Scripture:
"What I the Lord have spoken, I have spoken, and I excuse not myself; and though the heavens and the earth pass away, my word shall not pass away, but shall all be fulfilled, whether by mine own voice or by the voice of my servants, it is the same"
~D&C 1:38

Testimony:

"Let us in humility and faith refresh our dedication and our commitment to follow the prophets, seers, and revelators in all diligence. Let us listen and be instructed and edified by those who hold all the keys of the kingdom. And as we attend this conference, may our hearts be changed, that there will be a great desire to do good (see Alma 19:33), and that we will be pioneers in building a spiritual foundation that will establish the Church in our part of the world. In the name of Jesus Christ, amen."
~Elder Dieter F. Uchtdorf   October 2002

Quest #48
Choose the Right

Quote:

Choose the right! Choose the right!
Let wisdom mark the way before.
In its light, choose the right!
And God will bless you evermore.
~ *Joseph L. Townsend   Choose The Right (Hymns #239)*

"Now may I make a recommendation? Develop discipline of self so that, more and more, you do not have to decide and redecide what you will do when you are confronted with the same temptation time and time again. You need only to decide some things once. How great a blessing it is to be free of agonizing over and over again regarding a temptation. To do such is time-consuming and very risky.

Likewise, my dear young friends, the positive things you will want to accomplish need be decided upon only once—like going on a mission and living worthily in order to get married in the temple—and then all other decisions related to these goals can fall into line. Otherwise, each consideration is risky, and each equivocation may result in error. There are some things Latter-day Saints do and other things we just don't do. The sooner you take a stand, the taller you will be!"
~*President Spencer W. Kimball   President Kimball Speaks Out, (1981), 94.*

Experience:

On a recent trip to New Zealand, I met with a mission president who wore a beautiful tie tack with the inspiring CTR, or "Choose the Right," emblem. I had the impression that there must be a story behind this unique CTR pin. When I returned home, I wrote him a thank-you letter and asked him about his tie tack. I received this answer:

"You are very perceptive. Yes, there is a story behind the tie tack I'm wearing. I have a number of tie tacks I really prize. They have been gifts from my children, my wife, and friends. However, I choose to wear this beautiful silver shield inlaid with lovely blue turquoise, with the inspiring CTR emblem of our Primary.

"Why? I suppose it started back when I was a bishop and had an interview with a good-looking young man who was to receive the Aaronic Priesthood. He told me a special story. He related to me how one day after school, he and some of his friends found a package of cigarettes.

They decided to go down on the cliff alongside some large boulders and smoke them. They lit up, and the young man said that as he was looking down at the smoldering cigarette that he held between his fingers, he saw his CTR ring. He quickly put the cigarette out and made a very wise choice, never ever to do such a thing again. He chose to choose the right, as he remembered what the emblem stood for. From this story I gained a special love for the CTR emblem.

"Now for the story of how I came to be a recipient of the CTR tie tack. A few weeks ago before coming to New Zealand as a mission president, I was in the Kayenta Ward in Kayenta, Arizona. As I was saying some tender farewells to many of my Navajo friends, a remarkable young Navajo bishop gave me a big hug, then removed his tie tack and pinned it on my tie. As he did so, he asked me not to forget him.

"Now here in New Zealand, the last thing I do every morning as I dress for this great calling is to pin my tie tack with this beautiful silver and turquoise CTR emblem on my tie. I love it! It helps this old boilermaker make the right choices throughout the day. I know that it also helps fulfill the prophetic promise made to my wife and me from President Gordon B. Hinckley as he laid his hands on our heads and set us apart.

"He said words to this effect: 'You will have an instant bonding of love for every missionary in your mission.' I can't tell you how many times that a missionary, during a visit, has said something like this: 'President Gardner, I love your tie tack.' And then he or she will show me their CTR ring.

"I believe that Navajo bishop was inspired to give me the tie tack and that I make the right decision every day when I choose to wear it. And the beautiful blue and silver CTR pin is helping bond me to a royal army of missionaries in the New Zealand Wellington Mission.

"I appreciate the opportunity of relating to you my special experience associated with this great Primary children's motto, 'Choose the Right.'"
~Elder L. Tom Perry   October 1993

Scripture:
"...As for me and my house, we will serve the Lord"
~Joshua 24:15

Testimony:
"I promise you that you will receive everlasting happiness if you consistently choose to do what is right.

God lives! Jesus is the Christ! Obedience to His laws will lead us to life eternal is my solemn witness to you in the name of our Lord and Savior Jesus Christ, amen."

~Elder L. Tom Perry   October 1993

Quest #49
Pray Always

Quote:

"Morning and evening prayers—and all of the prayers in between—are not unrelated, discrete events; rather, they are linked together each day and across days, weeks, months, and even years. This is in part how we fulfill the scriptural admonition to "pray always". Such meaningful prayers are instrumental in obtaining the highest blessings God holds in store for His faithful children."

~Elder David A. Bednar   October 2008

Experience:

Many of us have had experiences with the sweet power of prayer. One of mine was shared with a stake patriarch from southern Utah. I first met him in my medical office more than 40 years ago, during the early pioneering days of surgery of the heart. This saintly soul suffered much because of a failing heart. He pleaded for help, thinking that his condition resulted from a damaged but repairable valve in his heart.

Extensive evaluation revealed that he had *two* faulty valves. While one could be helped surgically, the other could not. Thus, an operation was *not* advised. He received this news with deep disappointment. Subsequent visits ended with the same advice. Finally, in desperation, he spoke to me with considerable emotion: "Dr. Nelson, I have prayed for help and have been directed to you. The Lord will not reveal to me *how* to repair that second valve, but He can reveal it to you. Your mind is so prepared. If you will operate upon me, the Lord will make it known to you what to do. Please perform the operation that *I* need, and pray for the help that *you* need."

His great faith had a profound effect upon me. How could I turn him away again? Following a fervent prayer together, I agreed to try. In preparing for that fateful day, I prayed over and over again, but still did not know what to do for his leaking tricuspid valve. Even as the operation commenced, my assistant asked, "What are you going to do for that?" I said, "I do not know."

We began the operation. After relieving the obstruction of the first valve, we exposed the second valve. We found it to be intact but so badly dilated that it could no longer function as it should. While examining this valve, a message was distinctly impressed upon my mind: *Reduce the circumference of the ring.* I announced that message to my assistant. "The valve tissue will be sufficient *if* we can effectively reduce the ring toward its normal size."

But how? We could not apply a belt as one would use to tighten the waist of oversized trousers. We could not squeeze with a strap as one would cinch a saddle on a horse. Then a picture came vividly to my mind, showing how stitches could be placed—to make a pleat here and a tuck there—to accomplish the desired objective. I still remember that mental image—complete with dotted lines where sutures should be placed. The repair was completed as diagrammed in my mind. We tested the valve and found the leak to be reduced remarkably. My assistant said, "It's a miracle."

I responded, "It's an answer to prayer."
~President Russel M. Nelson   April 2003

Scripture:

"Watch ye therefore, and pray always, that ye may be accounted worthy to escape all these things that shall come to pass, and to stand before the Son of man."
~Luke 21:36

Testimony:

"I testify that there is a God in heaven who hears and answers prayers. I know this to be true, for He has answered mine. I would humbly urge all within the sound of my voice to keep in close touch with our Father in Heaven, through prayer."
~President Ezra Taft Benson   November 1982

Quest #50
Mothers

Quote:

"No love in mortality comes closer to approximating the pure love of Jesus Christ than the selfless love a devoted mother has for her child."
~Elder Jeffrey R. Holland   October 2015

"The love of a true mother comes nearer [to] being like the love of God than any other kind of love"
~President Joseph F. Smith   Improvement Era, Jan. 1910

"Women who make a house a home make a far greater contribution to society than those who command large armies or stand at the head of impressive corporations. Who can put a price tag on the influence a mother has on her children, a grandmother on her posterity, or aunts and sisters on their extended family?
~President Gordon B. Hinckley   Standing for Something   2000

Experience:

"As a boy, I well remember Sunday School on Mother's Day. We would hand to each mother present a small potted plant and sit in silent reverie as Melvin Watson, a blind member, would stand by the piano and sing, "That Wonderful Mother of Mine." This was the first time I saw a blind man cry. Even today, in memory, I can see the moist tears move from those sightless eyes, then form tiny rivulets and course down his cheeks, falling finally upon the lapel of the suit he had never seen. In boyhood puzzlement I wondered why all of the grown men were silent, why so many handkerchiefs came forth. Now I know. You see, mother was remembered. Each boy, every girl, all fathers and husbands seemed to make a silent pledge: "I will remember that wonderful mother of mine."
~President Thomas S. Monson

Scripture:

"Honour thy father and thy mother: that thy days may be long upon the land which the Lord thy God giveth thee."
~Exodus 20:12

Testimony:

"God bless you wonderful mothers and fathers in Zion. He has entrusted to your care His eternal children. As parents we partner, even join, with God in bringing to pass His work and glory among His children. It is our sacred duty to do our very best. Of this I testify in the name of Jesus Christ, amen.

~Elder L. Tom Perry   April 2010

Quest #51
Endure to the End

Quote:

"Regarding trials, including of our faith and patience, there are no exemptions—only variations (see Mosiah 23:21). These calisthenics are designed to increase our capacity for happiness and service. Yet the faithful will not be totally immune from the events on this planet. Thus the courageous attitudes of imperiled Shadrach, Meshach, and Abed-nego are worthy of emulation. They knew that God could rescue them. "But if not," they vowed, they would still serve God anyway (see Dan. 3:16–18)."

~Elder Neal A Maxwell   October 2002

"No pain that we suffer, no trial that we experience is wasted. It ministers to our education, to the development of such qualities as patience, faith, fortitude and humility. All that we suffer and all that we endure, especially when we endure it patiently, builds up our characters, purifies our hearts, expands our souls, and makes us more tender and charitable, more worthy to be called the children of God … and it is through sorrow and suffering, toil and tribulation, that we gain the education that we come here to acquire and which will make us more like our Father and Mother in heaven. …"

~Elder Orson F. Whitney

Experience:

"In about March 1946, less than a year after the end of the war, Ezra Taft Benson, then a member of the Quorum of the Twelve, accompanied by Frederick W. Babbel, was assigned a special postwar tour of Europe for the express purpose of meeting with the Saints, assessing their needs, and providing assistance to them. Elder Benson and Brother Babbel later recounted, from a testimony they heard, the experience of a Church member who found herself in an area no longer controlled by the government under which she had resided.

She and her husband had lived an idyllic life in East Prussia. Then had come the second great world war within their lifetimes. Her beloved young husband was killed during the final days of the frightful battles in their homeland, leaving her alone to care for their four children.

The occupying forces determined that the Germans in East Prussia must go to Western Germany to seek a new home. The woman was German, and so it was necessary for her to go. The journey was over a thousand miles (1,600 km), and she had no way to accomplish it but on foot. She was allowed to take only such bare necessities as she could load into her small wooden-wheeled wagon. Besides her children and these meager possessions, she took with her a strong faith in God and in the gospel as revealed to the latter-day prophet Joseph Smith.

She and the children began the journey in late summer. Having neither food nor money among her few possessions, she was forced to gather a daily subsistence from the fields and forests along the way. She was constantly faced with dangers from panic-stricken refugees and plundering troops.

As the days turned into weeks and the weeks to months, the temperatures dropped below freezing. Each day, she stumbled over the frozen ground, her smallest child—a baby—in her arms. Her three other children struggled along behind her, with the oldest—seven years old— pulling the tiny wooden wagon containing their belongings. Ragged and torn burlap was wrapped around their feet, providing the only protection for them, since their shoes had long since disintegrated. Their thin, tattered jackets covered their thin, tattered clothing, providing their only protection against the cold.

Soon the snows came, and the days and nights became a nightmare. In the evenings she and the children would try to find some kind of shelter— a barn or a shed—and would huddle together for warmth, with a few thin blankets from the wagon on top of them.

She constantly struggled to force from her mind overwhelming fears that they would perish before reaching their destination.

And then one morning the unthinkable happened. As she awakened, she felt a chill in her heart. The tiny form of her three-year-old daughter was cold and still, and she realized that death had claimed the child. Though overwhelmed with grief, she knew that she must take the other children and travel on. First, however, she used the only implement she had—a tablespoon—to dig a grave in the frozen ground for her tiny, precious child.

Death, however, was to be her companion again and again on the journey. Her seven-year-old son died, either from starvation or from freezing or both. Again her only shovel was the tablespoon, and again she dug hour after hour to lay his mortal remains gently into the earth. Next, her five-year-old son died, and again she used her tablespoon as a shovel.

Her despair was all consuming. She had only her tiny baby daughter left, and the poor thing was failing. Finally, as she was reaching the end of her journey, the baby died in her arms. The spoon was gone now, so hour after hour she dug a grave in the frozen earth with her bare fingers. Her grief became unbearable. How could she possibly be kneeling in the snow at the graveside of her last child? She had lost her husband and all her children. She had given up her earthly goods, her home, and even her homeland.

In this moment of overwhelming sorrow and complete bewilderment, she felt her heart would literally break. In despair she contemplated how she might end her own life, as so many of her fellow countrymen were doing. How easy it would be to jump off a nearby bridge, she thought, or to throw herself in front of an oncoming train.

And then, as these thoughts assailed her, something within her said, "Get down on your knees and pray." She ignored the prompting until she could resist it no longer. She knelt and prayed more fervently than she had in her entire life:

"Dear Heavenly Father, I do not know how I can go on. I have nothing left—except my faith in Thee. I feel, Father, amidst the desolation of my soul, an overwhelming gratitude for the atoning sacrifice of Thy Son, Jesus Christ. I cannot express adequately my love for Him. I know that because He suffered and died, I shall live again with my family; that because He broke the chains of death, I shall see my children again and will have the joy of raising them. Though I do not at this moment wish to live, I will do so, that we may be reunited as a family and return—together—to Thee."

When she finally reached her destination of Karlsruhe, Germany, she was emaciated. Brother Babbel said that her face was a purple-gray, her eyes red and swollen, her joints protruding. She was literally in the advanced stages of starvation. In a Church meeting shortly thereafter, she bore a glorious testimony, stating that of all the ailing people in her saddened land, she was one of the happiest because she knew that God lived, that Jesus is the Christ, and that He died and was resurrected so that we might live again. She testified that she knew if she continued faithful and true to the end, she would be reunited with those she had lost and would be saved in the celestial kingdom of God.

From the holy scriptures we read, "Behold, the righteous, the saints of the Holy One of Israel, they who have believed in [Him], they who have endured the crosses of the world, ... they shall inherit the kingdom of God, ... and their joy shall be full forever."

~President Thomas S. Monson   April 2009

Scripture:

"And, if you keep my commandments and endure to the end you shall have eternal life, which gift is the greatest of all the gifts of God."
~Doctrine and Covenants 14:7

Testimony:

"There are people who are bitter as they watch loved ones suffer agonies and interminable pain and physical torture. Some would charge the Lord with unkindness, indifference, and injustice. We are so incompetent to judge! ...

The power of the priesthood is limitless but God has wisely placed upon each of us certain limitations. I may develop priesthood power as I perfect my life, yet I am grateful that even through the priesthood I cannot heal all the sick. I might heal people who should die. I might relieve people of suffering who should suffer. I fear I would frustrate the purposes of God. Had I limitless power, and yet limited vision and understanding, I might have saved Abinadi from the flames of fire when he was burned at the stake, and in doing so I might have irreparably damaged him. He died a martyr and went to a martyr's reward⸺—exaltation.

I would likely have protected Paul against his woes if my power were boundless. I would surely have healed his "thorn in the flesh."
[2 Corinthians 12:7.] And in doing so I might have foiled the Lord's program. Thrice he offered prayers, asking the Lord to remove the "thorn" from him, but the Lord did not so answer his prayers [see 2 Corinthians 12:7–10]. Paul many times could have lost himself if he had been eloquent, well, handsome, and free from the things that made him humble. ...

I fear that had I been in Carthage Jail on June 27, 1844, I might have deflected the bullets that pierced the body of the Prophet and the Patriarch. I might have saved them from the sufferings and agony, but lost to them the martyr's death and reward. I am glad I did not have to make that decision.

With such uncontrolled power, I surely would have felt to protect Christ from the agony in Gethsemane, the insults, the thorny crown, the indignities in the court, the physical injuries. I would have administered to his wounds and healed them, giving him cooling water instead of vinegar. I might have saved him from suffering and death, and lost to the world his atoning sacrifice.

I would not dare to take the responsibility of bringing back to life my loved ones. Christ himself acknowledged the difference between his will and the Father's when he prayed that the cup of suffering be taken from him; yet he added, "Nevertheless, not my will but thine be done." [Luke 22:42.]

~President Spencer W. Kimball   Faith Precedes the Miracle, (1972), 97-100

Quest #52
Hold Fast to the Iron Rod

Quote:

"The forces of good are clearly and continually under attack. There are times when it seems the world is almost drowning in a flood of filth and degradation. And I want to cry out, "Hold on! Hold on to what is right and true. Therein is safety. Don't let yourself be swept away."

~*President Spencer W. Kimball   October 1978*

Experience:

"In the fall of 2001 three of the Twelve were in Brazil at the same time, and each taught the promises of an honest tithing. A few months later a young college student in Sao Paulo was put to the test. She was working and going to school. Here are her words, which were shared by President Hinckley:

The university in which I studied had a regulation that prohibited the students [who had not paid all their fees] *from taking tests. . .*

I . . . faced serious financial difficulties. It was a Thursday when I received my salary. When I figured the monthly budget, I noticed that there wouldn't be enough to pay [both] *my tithing and my university. I would have to choose between them. The bimonthly tests would start the following week, and if I didn't take them I could lose the school year. I felt great agony. . . . My heart ached. I had a painful decision before me, and I didn't know what to decide.*

Through prayer she determined that she would trust in the Lord and in the words of the prophets. On Sunday she paid her tithing. The next day she sought a way to be able to take her tests but could not find a solution. She then explained what happened:

The working period was ending when my employer approached and gave the last orders of the day. . . . Suddenly, he halted, and . . . asked, "How is your college?" I was surprised. . . . The only thing I could answer . . . was, "Everything is all right!" He looked thoughtfully at me and bid farewell again. . . .

Suddenly the secretary entered the room, saying that I was a very fortunate person! When I asked her why, she simply answered: "The employer has just said that from today on the company is going to pay fully for your college and your books. Before you leave, stop at my desk and inform me of the costs so that tomorrow I can give you the check."

The student then explained her feelings:

After [the secretary] *left, crying and feeling very humble, I knelt exactly where I was and thanked the Lord for His generosity. I . . . said to Heavenly Father that He didn't have to bless me so much. I only needed the cost of one month's installment, and the tithing I had paid on Sunday was very small compared to the amount I was receiving! During that prayer the words recorded in Malachi* [and declared so often by the prophets and apostles] *came to my mind: "Prove me now herewith, saith the Lord of hosts, if I will not open you the windows of heaven, and pour you out a blessing, that there shall not be room enough to receive it" (Mal. 3:10).*

Clouded in the mists of darkness, the decision was difficult; the outcome was unsure. But she held fast to the iron rod. Her faith in the Lord and in the Lord's prophets was confirmed. While all experiences may not be so immediate in their resolution, the promises for those who honestly keep the law of tithing are absolutely certain."

~Elder Neil L. Andersen   March 2007

Scripture:

"And now, my sons, remember, remember that it is upon the rock of our Redeemer, who is Christ, the Son of God, that ye must build your foundation; that when the devil shall send forth his mighty winds, yea, his shafts in the whirlwind, yea, when all his hail and his mighty storm shall beat upon you, it shall have no power over you to drag you down to the gulf of misery and endless wo, because of the rock upon which ye are built, which is a sure foundation, a foundation whereon if men build they cannot fall."

~Helaman 5:12

Testimony:

"The Lord holds forth a glorious promise to those who love him and demonstrate this love by faithful, devoted service and the living of his eternal principles. When the winds of change blow fiercely and the waves sweep over us, we have a tree or rod of principle to which we can cling for safety. It is the gospel of Jesus Christ which has been restored to the earth in its fulness.

May the Lord bless us, each one, to hold fast to the iron rod, I humbly pray, in the name of Jesus Christ. Amen."

~President Spencer W. Kimball   October 1978

Quest #53
Joseph Smith

Quote:

"Joseph Smith, the Prophet and Seer of the Lord, has done more, save Jesus only, for the salvation of men in this world, than any other man that ever lived in it."

~President John Taylor   Doctrine and Covenants 135:3

Experience:

"The church was organized on the 6th of April, 1830, with six members, but Joseph had faith that the kingdom thus commenced, like a grain of mustard seed, would become a great church and kingdom upon the earth.

Joseph Smith was what he professed to be, a prophet of God, a seer and revelator. He laid the foundation of this church and kingdom, and lived long enough to deliver the keys of the kingdom to the elders of Israel, unto the twelve apostles. He spent the last winter of his life, some three or four months, with the quorum of the twelve, teaching them. It was not merely a few hours ministering to them the ordinances of the gospel; but he spent day after day, week after week and month after month, teaching them and a few others the things of the kingdom of God.

Elder Wilford Woodruff was present when the Prophet Joseph Smith gave the keys of the kingdom to the Quorum of the Twelve Apostles.

For some time before his death the Prophet Joseph was inspired of the Lord to anticipate his own departure from earthly scenes. This was shown in various ways; but especially in the great anxiety which he displayed to bestow upon the Twelve Apostles all the keys and authority of the Holy Priesthood which he had received. He declared in private and in public that they were equipped and fully qualified, and that he had rolled the kingdom of God on to the shoulders of the Twelve Apostles.

"I, Wilford Woodruff, being the last man living in the flesh who was present upon that occasion, feel it a duty I owe to the Church of Jesus Christ of Latter-day Saints, to the House of Israel, and to the whole world, to bear this my last testimony to all nations, that in the winter of 1843–4, Joseph Smith, the Prophet of God, called the Twelve Apostles together in the City of Nauvoo, and spent many days with us in giving us our endowments, and teaching us those glorious principles which God had revealed to him. And upon one occasion he stood upon his feet in our midst for nearly three hours, declaring unto us the great and last dispensation which God had set His hand to perform upon the earth in these last days. The room was filled as if with consuming fire; the Prophet was clothed upon with much of the power of God, and his face shone and was transparently clear, and he closed that speech, never-to-be-forgotten in time or in eternity, with the following language:

"Brethren, I have had great sorrow of heart for fear that I might be taken from the earth with the keys of the kingdom of God upon me, without sealing them upon the heads of other men. God has sealed upon my head all the keys of the kingdom of God necessary for organizing and building up of the Church, Zion, and kingdom of God upon the earth, and to prepare the Saints for the coming of the Son of Man. Now, brethren, I thank God I have lived to see the day that I have been enabled to give you your endowments, and I have now sealed upon your heads all the powers of the Aaronic and Melchizedec priesthoods and apostleship, with all the keys and powers thereof, which God has sealed upon me; and I now roll off all the labor, burden and care of this Church and kingdom of God upon your shoulders, and I now command you in the name of the Lord Jesus Christ to round up your shoulders, and bear off this Church and kingdom of God before heaven and earth, and before God, angels and men; and if you don't do it you will be damned."

And the same Spirit that filled the room at that time burns in my bosom while I record this testimony."

~President Wilford Woodruff

Scripture:

"The ends of the earth shall inquire after thy name, and fools shall have thee in derision, and hell shall rage against thee;

While the pure in heart, and the wise, and the noble, and the virtuous, shall seek counsel, and authority, and blessings constantly from under thy hand.

And thy people shall never be turned against thee by the testimony of traitors.

And although their influence shall cast thee into trouble, and into bars and walls, thou shalt be had in honor; and but for a small moment and thy voice shall be more terrible in the midst of thine enemies than the fierce lion, because of thy righteousness; and thy God shall stand by thee forever and ever.

If thou art called to pass through tribulation; if thou art in perils among false brethren; if thou art in perils among robbers; if thou art in perils by land or by sea;

If thou art accused with all manner of false accusations; if thine enemies fall upon thee; if they tear thee from the society of thy father and mother and brethren and sisters; and if with a drawn sword thine enemies tear thee from the bosom of thy wife, and of thine offspring, and thine elder son, although but six years of age, shall cling to thy garments, and shall say, My father, my father, why can't you stay with us? O, my father, what are the men going to do with you? and if then he shall be thrust from thee by the sword, and thou be dragged to prison, and thine enemies prowl around thee like wolves for the blood of the lamb;

And if thou shouldst be cast into the pit, or into the hands of murderers, and the sentence of death passed upon thee; if thou be cast into the deep; if the billowing surge conspire against thee; if fierce winds become thine enemy; if the heavens gather blackness, and all the elements combine to hedge up the way; and above all, if the very jaws of hell shall gape open the mouth wide after thee, know thou, my son, that all these things shall give thee experience, and shall be for thy good.

The Son of Man hath descended below them all. Art thou greater than he?

Therefore, hold on thy way, and the priesthood shall remain with thee; for their bounds are set, they cannot pass. Thy days are known, and thy years shall not be numbered less; therefore, fear not what man can do, for God shall be with you forever and ever."

~D&C 122 : 1-9

Testimony:

"His office is not taken from him, he has only gone to labor in another department of the operations of the Almighty. He is still an Apostle, still a Prophet, and is doing the work of an Apostle and Prophet; he has gone one step beyond us and gained a victory that you and I have not gained (DBY, 468).

"I know that [Joseph Smith] was called of God, and this I know by the revelations of Jesus Christ to me, and by the testimony of the Holy Ghost. Had I not so learned this truth, I should never have been what is called a "Mormon," neither should I have been here to-day (DNW, 22 Oct. 1862, 2).

~President Brigham Young

Quest #54
Serving Each Other

Quote:

"We are surrounded by those in need of our attention, our encouragement, our support, our comfort, our kindness—be they family members, friends, acquaintances, or strangers. We are the Lord's hands here upon the earth, with the mandate to serve and to lift His children. He is dependent upon each of us."

-President Thomas S. Monson   October 2009

Experience:

"An old Jewish legend tells of two brothers, Abram and Zimri, who owned a field and worked it together. They agreed to divide both the labor and the harvest equally. One night as the harvest came to a close, Zimri could not sleep, for it didn't seem right that Abram, who had a wife and seven sons to feed, should receive only half of the harvest, while he, with only himself to support, had so much.

So Zimri dressed and quietly went into the field, where he took a third of his harvest and put it in his brother's pile. He then returned to his bed, satisfied that he had done the right thing.

Meanwhile, Abram could not sleep either. He thought of his poor brother, Zimri, who was all alone and had no sons to help him with the work. It did not seem right that Zimri, who worked so hard by himself, should get only half of the harvest. Surely this was not pleasing to God. And so Abram quietly went to the fields, where he took a third of his harvest and placed it in the pile of his beloved brother.

The next morning, the brothers went to the field and were both astonished that the piles still looked to be the same size. That night both brothers slipped out of their houses to repeat their efforts of the previous night. But this time they discovered each other, and when they did, they wept and embraced.   Neither could speak, for their hearts were overcome with love and gratitude.

This is the spirit of compassion: that we love others as ourselves, seek their happiness, and do unto them as we hope they would do unto us."

~President Dieter F. Uchtdorf   April 2010

Scripture:

"Verily I say unto you, Inasmuch as ye have done it unto one of the least of these my brethren, ye have done it unto me."

~Matthew 25:40

Testimony:

"Just before the Savior's Crucifixion, He taught His Apostles: "A new commandment I give unto you, That ye love one another; as I have loved you" and "If ye love me, keep my commandments."

"I testify that the Savior's true posture toward us is the one posed by the outstretched arms of Thorvaldsen's statue Christus. He continues to stretch forth His hands, beckoning, "Come, follow me." We follow Him by loving and serving one another and keeping His commandments."
~Elder Robert D. Hales   October 2016

Quest #55
Keeping the Sabbath Holy

Quote:

"The Sabbath is a holy day in which to do worthy and holy things. Abstinence from work and recreation is important but insufficient. The Sabbath calls for constructive thoughts and acts, and if one merely lounges about doing nothing on the Sabbath, he is breaking it. To observe it, one will be on his knees in prayer, preparing lessons, studying the gospel, meditating, visiting the ill and distressed, sleeping, reading wholesome material, and attending all the meetings of that day to which he is expected. To fail to do these proper things is a transgression on the omission side."

-President Spencer W. Kimball   The Miracle of Forgiveness, (1969), 96-97

Experience:

"Some time ago I was assigned to a conference in northern Utah in June. As I drove through Cache Valley on Saturday, I was struck by the beauty of that peaceful green valley. I marveled at the temple in Logan—such a serene, peaceful beacon in so many ways. As I continued north on that clear summer day, I was impressed with the green fields so rich with a variety of crops. I particularly noticed the great number of alfalfa fields and the constant activity in nearly all of them. What a pleasing sensation it was to smell that freshly mown hay and to see the straight rows and the orderly cutting of those meticulously groomed fields.

I pulled the car over to the side of the road at the top of one of the hills and got out. I found myself absorbed right into that beautiful valley. As far as I could see was a whole panorama of the same activity in every direction—hay being mowed and stacked and hauled.

I finally drove on to the stake where we had a wonderful conference.

My parents live in southeast Idaho, and since I was already more than halfway there, I decided to drive up Sunday afternoon to visit them before returning home.

So, after conference I started north through the rest of Cache Valley. Within a few miles I was in Idaho, but the scenery and feeling were just the same. I again became absorbed in the beauty of the green fields and the smell of fresh hay all around. Again, I stopped at the top of one of the hills and got out and looked as far as I could in all directions. It was just as beautiful—if not more so—than the day before. "Yes, even more beautiful," I thought, "but why?" The sun and sky and the clouds and the fields were all the same. Why this deep feeling that this sight this Sunday afternoon was even more beautiful than the day before?

What was the difference? I noticed in the distance a small LDS chapel and a few cars starting to pull up to it. Then it struck me, rather peacefully but very effectively: "There is the difference. No one is mowing or hauling hay today." I looked as far as I could and saw hay fields everywhere, tractors stopped, mowing machines idle, and trucks resting in the fields, but no one working—for it was the Sabbath and this was Cache Valley and these were largely good Latter-day Saint people.

As I continued north, I saw everywhere hay to be cut and stacked and hauled and equipment and weather to do it, but no man or woman in the fields. The people of this valley were observing a higher law, and the Sabbath was being kept holy in Cache Valley.

I went by dozens, even hundreds, of farms with machines waiting in the fields—left Saturday evening by God-fearing men waiting for Monday to come and the whine of activity to resume. I wondered to myself, "Will someone break this spell, will someone be out in his fields working?"

Each time I rounded a corner or came to the top of a hill, I would look and look and then breathe a sigh of relief—no one working.

I went farther and farther north, realizing I was near the end of this beautiful valley. "Would anyone break the spell? Could it be a whole valley so dedicated to God that no one would work on the Sabbath?" The suspense became almost unbearable. Each curve I rounded or each hill I came over found me looking in almost fearful anticipation, then smiling as the same peaceful scene continued.

Finally I came to the last curve and the confluence with the main road that marked the end of Cache Valley. I looked and looked, but all was peaceful and quiet. I was so excited, I pulled the car over, got out, and in almost a Toyota-like jump I raised my hands and shouted, "You did it, Cache Valley. You did it! I have traversed your length. You didn't know I was looking, but you did it—not one field being mowed, not one tractor at work, not one truck hauling. You did it!" (I recognize that I had been through only the northern end of the valley that Sunday, but it was still Cache Valley.)

I instinctively looked heavenward and said, "Did you see that? Did you see Cache Valley this Sunday afternoon?"

Even though I didn't hear anything, it was as though I sensed a response saying, "Yes, we know. We see everything."

~Elder John H. Groberg   October 1984

Scripture:

"If thou turn away thy foot from the sabbath, from doing thy pleasure on my holy day; and call the sabbath a delight, the holy of the Lord, honourable; and shalt honour him, not doing thine own ways, nor finding thine own pleasure, nor speaking thine own words:

Then shalt thou delight thyself in the Lord; and I will cause thee to ride upon the high places of the earth, and feed thee with the heritage of Jacob thy father: for the mouth of the Lord hath spoken it."
~Isaiah 58:13-14

Testimony:

"On this day before the Sabbath, as we begin this great conference, let us remember the blessings and opportunities that are ours as we attend sacrament meeting each week in our wards and branches. Let us prepare and conduct ourselves on the Sabbath in a manner that will call down the blessings promised us upon ourselves and our families. I bear my special witness that the greatest joy we receive in this life is in following the Savior. May we keep His commandments by keeping His sacred day holy is my prayer in the name of Jesus Christ, amen."
~Elder L. Tom Perry   April 2011

Quest #56
Gratitude

Quote:

"When you walk with gratitude, you do not walk with arrogance and conceit and egotism, you walk with a spirit of thanksgiving that is becoming to you and will bless your lives."
~*President Gordon B. Hinckley   Teachings of Gordon B. Hinckley, (1997), 250*

Experience:

"I share with you an account of one family which was able to find blessings in the midst of serious challenges. This is an account I read many years ago and have kept because of the message it conveys. It was written by Gordon Green and appeared in an American magazine over 50 years ago.

Gordon tells how he grew up on a farm in Canada, where he and his siblings had to hurry home from school while the other children played ball and went swimming. Their father, however, had the capacity to help them understand that their work amounted to something. This was especially true after harvesttime when the family celebrated Thanksgiving, for on that day their father gave them a great gift. He took an inventory of everything they had.

On Thanksgiving morning he would take them to the cellar with its barrels of apples, bins of beets, carrots packed in sand, and mountains of sacked potatoes as well as peas, corn, string beans, jellies, strawberries, and other preserves which filled their shelves. He had the children count everything carefully. Then they went out to the barn and figured how many tons of hay there were and how many bushels of grain in the granary. They counted the cows, pigs, chickens, turkeys, and geese. Their father said he wanted to see how they stood, but they knew he really wanted them to realize on that feast day how richly God had blessed them and had smiled upon all their hours of work. Finally, when they sat down to the feast their mother had prepared, the blessings were something they felt.

Gordon indicated, however, that the Thanksgiving he remembered most thankfully was the year they seemed to have nothing for which to be grateful.

The year started off well: they had leftover hay, lots of seed, four litters of pigs, and their father had a little money set aside so that someday he could afford to buy a hay loader—a wonderful machine most farmers just dreamed of owning. It was also the year that electricity came to their town—although not to them because they couldn't afford it.

One night when Gordon's mother was doing her big wash, his father stepped in and took his turn over the washboard and asked his wife to rest and do her knitting. He said, "You spend more time doing the wash than sleeping. Do you think we should break down and get electricity?" Although elated at the prospect, she shed a tear or two as she thought of the hay loader that wouldn't be bought.

So the electrical line went up their lane that year. Although it was nothing fancy, they acquired a washing machine that worked all day by itself and brilliant lightbulbs that dangled from each ceiling. There were no more lamps to fill with oil, no more wicks to cut, no more sooty chimneys to wash. The lamps went quietly off to the attic.

The coming of electricity to their farm was almost the last good thing that happened to them that year. Just as their crops were starting to come through the ground, the rains started. When the water finally receded, there wasn't a plant left anywhere. They planted again, but more rains beat the crops into the earth. Their potatoes rotted in the mud. They sold a couple of cows and all the pigs and other livestock they had intended to keep, getting very low prices for them because everybody else had to do the same thing. All they harvested that year was a patch of turnips which had somehow weathered the storms.

Then it was Thanksgiving again. Their mother said, "Maybe we'd better forget it this year. We haven't even got a goose left."

On Thanksgiving morning, however, Gordon's father showed up with a jackrabbit and asked his wife to cook it. Grudgingly she started the job, indicating it would take a long time to cook that tough old thing. When it was finally on the table with some of the turnips that had survived, the children refused to eat. Gordon's mother cried, and then his father did a strange thing. He went up to the attic, got an oil lamp, took it back to the table, and lighted it. He told the children to turn out the electric lights. When there was only the lamp again, they could hardly believe that it had been that dark before. They wondered how they had ever seen anything without the bright lights made possible by electricity.

The food was blessed, and everyone ate. When dinner was over, they all sat quietly. Wrote Gordon:
"In the humble dimness of the old lamp we were beginning to see clearly again. ...
"It [was] a lovely meal. The jack rabbit tasted like turkey and the turnips were the mildest we could recall. ...

"… [Our] home …, for all its want, was so rich [to] us."
~*President Thomas S. Monson   October 2010*

Scripture:

"I say unto you, my brethren, that if you should render all
the thanks and praise which your whole soul has power to possess, to that
God who has created you, and has kept and preserved you, and has
caused that ye should rejoice, and has granted that ye should live in peace
one with another—

I say unto you that if ye should serve him who has created you from the
beginning, and is preserving you from day to day, by lending you breath,
that ye may live and move and do according to your own will, and even
supporting you from one moment to another—I say, if ye should serve
him with all your whole souls yet ye would be unprofitable servants."
~*Mosiah 2:20-21*

Testimony:

"Thou shalt thank the Lord thy God in all things." (D&C 59:7.)

This scripture means that we express thankfulness for what happens,
not only for the good things in life but also for the opposition and
challenges of life that add to our experience and faith. We put our lives in
His hands, realizing that all that transpires will be for our experience.

When in prayer we say, "Thy will be done," we are really expressing
faith and gratitude and acknowledging that we will accept whatever
happens in our lives.

That we may feel true gratitude for the goodness of God for all the
blessings that have been given to us and express those feelings of
thankfulness in prayer to our Heavenly Father is my prayer in the name of
Jesus Christ, amen."
~*Elder Robert D. Hales   April 1992*

Quest #57
Forgiveness

Quote:

Let me live in a house by the side of the road
Where the race of men go by-
The men who are good and the men who are bad,
As good and as bad as I.

I would not sit in the scorner's seat
Nor hurl the cynic's ban-
Let me live in a house by the side of the road
And be a friend to man.
~Sam Walter Foss

Experience:

   "In the beautiful hills of Pennsylvania, a devout group of Christian people live a simple life without automobiles, electricity, or modern machinery. They work hard and live quiet, peaceful lives separate from the world. Most of their food comes from their own farms. The women sew and knit and weave their clothing, which is modest and plain. They are known as the Amish people.

   A 32-year-old milk truck driver lived with his family in their Nickel Mines community. He was not Amish, but his pickup route took him to many Amish dairy farms, where he became known as the quiet milkman. Last October he suddenly lost all reason and control. In his tormented mind he blamed God for the death of his first child and some unsubstantiated memories. He stormed into the Amish school without any provocation, released the boys and adults, and tied up the 10 girls. He shot the girls, killing five and wounding five. Then he took his own life.

   This shocking violence caused great anguish among the Amish but no anger. There was hurt but no hate. Their forgiveness was immediate. Collectively they began to reach out to the milkman's suffering family. As the milkman's family gathered in his home the day after the shootings, an Amish neighbor came over, wrapped his arms around the father of the dead gunman, and said, "We will forgive you." Amish leaders visited the milkman's wife and children to extend their sympathy, their forgiveness, their help, and their love. About half of the mourners at the milkman's funeral were Amish. In turn, the Amish invited the milkman's family to attend the funeral services of the girls who had been killed. A remarkable peace settled on the Amish as their faith sustained them during this crisis.

One local resident very eloquently summed up the aftermath of this tragedy when he said, "We were all speaking the same language, and not just English, but a language of caring, a language of community, [and] a language of service. And, yes, a language of forgiveness." It was an amazing outpouring of their complete faith in the Lord's teachings in the Sermon on the Mount: "Do good to them that hate you, and pray for them which despitefully use you."

The family of the milkman who killed the five girls released the following statement to the public:

"To our Amish friends, neighbors, and local community:

"Our family wants each of you to know that we are overwhelmed by the forgiveness, grace, and mercy that you've extended to us. Your love for our family has helped to provide the healing we so desperately need. The prayers, flowers, cards, and gifts you've given have touched our hearts in a way no words can describe. Your compassion has reached beyond our family, beyond our community, and is changing our world, and for this we sincerely thank you.

"Please know that our hearts have been broken by all that has happened. We are filled with sorrow for all of our Amish neighbors whom we have loved and continue to love. We know that there are many hard days ahead for all the families who lost loved ones, and so we will continue to put our hope and trust in the God of all comfort, as we all seek to rebuild our lives."

How could the whole Amish group manifest such an expression of forgiveness? It was because of their faith in God and trust in His word, which is part of their inner beings. They see themselves as disciples of Christ and want to follow His example.

Hearing of this tragedy, many people sent money to the Amish to pay for the health care of the five surviving girls and for the burial expenses of the five who were killed. As a further demonstration of their discipleship, the Amish decided to share some of the money with the widow of the milkman and her three children because they too were victims of this terrible tragedy.

~President James E Faust   April 2007

Scripture:

"For verily, verily I say unto you, he that hath the spirit of contention is not of me, but is of the devil, who is the father of contention, and he stirreth up the hearts of men to contend with anger, one with another.

Behold, this is not my doctrine, to stir up the hearts of men with anger, one against another; but this is my doctrine, that such things should be done away.

~3 Nephi 11:29-30

Testimony:

"May God help us to be a little kinder, showing forth greater forbearance, to be more forgiving, more willing to walk the second mile, to reach down and lift up those who may have sinned but have brought forth the fruits of repentance, to lay aside old grudges and nurture them no more. For this I humbly pray, in the sacred name of our Redeemer, even the Lord Jesus Christ, amen."

~President Gordon B. Hinckley   October 2005

Quest #58
Freedom

Quote:

"...those men who laid the foundation of this American government and signed the Declaration of Independence were the best spirits the God of heaven could find on the face of the earth. They were choice spirits, not wicked men. General Washington and all the men who labored for the purpose were inspired of the Lord."

~Wilford Woodruff   April 1898

O beautiful for heroes proved
In liberating strife,
Who more than self their country loved,
And mercy more than life!

~ Katherine Lee Bates   *(America the Beautiful, ver. 3)*

Experience:

"I want to tell you of a faithful brother who was a member of the same branch in my home country of Germany in the early years of my membership.

He was living in humble circumstances and felt very blessed to have recently begun a job in a small, privately owned company. He told me about an upcoming event where all of the employed people were invited to participate in a traditional company dinner party. He was concerned because he knew that there would be a big beer party at the end of this meeting, with the boss being probably the heaviest beer drinker of them all. But he also knew that it would be considered very impolite if he did not attend the dinner at all.

When I saw him again, after that dinner event occurred, I saw him with a most happy, deep inner glow, and he could not wait to tell me what had happened. Because he was new in the company, the boss had sat right next to him, wanting to get to know him better. As the evening progressed, the brother saw his wildest fears confirmed because the boss would not tolerate that he would not drink beer with him, and he said, "What kind of church is that that would not permit you to drink even a glass of beer with me?"

The fear of my friend did not grow into panic as he was able to calmly answer his boss that the reason he was not drinking had nothing to do with the church that he belonged to, but that *he* himself had made a sacred covenant with God that he would not drink. If he would ever break this covenant, how could he continue to stay true to that which he would ever promise, and how could he be trusted, even by his employer, that he would not lie or steal or cheat.

According to my friend, the owner was deeply touched by this statement, and he hugged him, speaking words of profound admiration and confidence.

My dear brothers and sisters, in The Church of Jesus Christ of Latter-day Saints, many new members, specifically when they come from countries other than the United States, learn for the first time the true dimension of the word *freedom.* Freedom for most people of the world means "freedom from" the absence of malice or pain or suppression. But the freedom that God means when He deals with us goes one step further. He means "freedom to"—the freedom to act in the dignity of our own choice."

~Elder F. Enzio Busche   October 2000

Scripture:

"And ye shall know the truth, and the truth shall make you free."
~John 8: 32

Testimony:

"There should be no doubt what our task is today. If we truly cherish the heritage we have received, we must maintain the same virtues and the same character of our stalwart forebears—faith in God, courage, industry, frugality, self-reliance, and integrity. We have the obligation to maintain what those who pledged their lives, their fortunes, and sacred honor gave to future generations. Our opportunity and obligation for doing so is clearly upon us.

As one with you, charged with the responsibility of protecting and perpetuating this noble heritage, I stand today with bowed head and heart overflowing with gratitude. May we begin to repay this debt by preserving and strengthening this heritage in our own lives, in the lives of our children, their children, and generations yet unborn. In the name of Jesus Christ. Amen."

~President Ezra Taft Benson   October 1976

Quest #59
Blessings of Prayer

Quote:

"All through my life the counsel to depend on prayer has been prized above almost any other advice I have received. It has become an integral part of me, an anchor, a constant source of strength, and the basis for my knowledge of things divine."
~ *President Ezra Taft Benson   April 1977*

Experience:

"I always have very tender feelings about prayers and the power and blessings of prayer," said President Spencer W. Kimball. "In my lifetime I have received more blessings than I can ever adequately give thanks for. The Lord has been so good to me. I have had so many experiences in sickness and in health that leave me with no shadow of doubt in my heart and mind that there is a God in heaven, that he is our Father, and that he hears and answers our prayers."

One of these experiences came when President Kimball and his wife, Camilla, traveled to a conference in New Zealand. When they reached the city of Hamilton, they were so sick that President Kimball asked President N. Eldon Tanner, First Counselor in the First Presidency, to represent him at a cultural event planned for that evening. Some hours later, President Kimball "awakened with a start and asked Dr. Russell Nelson, who sat watching over him, 'Brother Nelson, what time was that program to begin this evening?'

"'At seven o'clock, President Kimball.'

"'What time is it now?'

"'It is almost seven.'

"Spencer was soaked with perspiration. His fever had broken. ... He said, 'Tell Sister Kimball we're going.'

"Camilla got out of bed, and they both hurriedly dressed and then drove the short distance to the stadium where the program had just convened. President Tanner had explained at the beginning of the meeting that they were too sick to attend. In the opening prayer a young New Zealander petitioned fervently, 'We three thousand New Zealand youth have gathered here prepared to sing and to dance for thy prophet. Wilt thou heal him and deliver him here.' As the prayer ended, the car carrying Spencer and Camilla entered and the stadium erupted in a spontaneous, deafening shout at the answer to their prayer."

~Spencer W. Kimball   Camilla: A Biography of Camilla Eyring Kimball (1980), 182–84

Scripture:

"Counsel with the Lord in all thy doings, and he will direct thee for good; yea, when thou liest down at night lie down unto the Lord, that he may watch over you in your sleep; and when thou risest in the morning let thy heart be full of thanks unto God; and if ye do these things, ye shall be lifted up at the last day."

~Alma 37:37

Testimony:

"I testify that prayer becomes more meaningful as we counsel with the Lord in all of our doings, as we express heartfelt gratitude, and as we pray for others with real intent and a sincere heart.

I witness Heavenly Father lives and that He hears and answers every earnest prayer. Jesus is the Christ, our Savior and Mediator. Revelation is real. The fulness of the gospel has been restored to the earth in this dispensation. I so testify in the sacred name of the Lord Jesus Christ, amen."

~ Elder David A. Bednar   October 2008

Quest #60
Testimony of Jesus Christ

Quote:

"I have been buoyed up and, as it were, lifted out of myself and given power not my own to teach the glorious truths proclaimed by the Redeemer of the world. I have not seen Him face to face but have enjoyed the companionship of His spirit and felt His presence in a way not to be mistaken. I know that my Redeemer lives and gladly yield my humble efforts to establish His teachings. ... Every fibre of my being vibrates with the knowledge that He lives and some day all men will know it.

"The Savior died that we might live. He overcame death and the grave and holds out to all who obey His teachings the hope of a glorious resurrection. ... I know this is the work of the Lord, that Jesus was indeed our Savior."

~ President George Albert Smith   Testimony of Elder George Albert Smith, Liahona: The Elders' Journal, Feb. 2, 1915, 502

Experience:

"On 4 December 1920, Elder David O. McKay and his traveling companion, Hugh J. Cannon, a stake president and editor of the Church magazine the Improvement Era, began an assignment from the First Presidency to visit and strengthen Church members throughout the world. Their trip lasted one year and took them approximately 60,000 miles, over half that distance traveled on water. On the evening of 10 May 1921, as they sailed toward what is now Western Samoa, Elder McKay had the following experience:

"Toward evening, the reflection of the afterglow of a beautiful sunset was most splendid! ... Pondering still upon this beautiful scene, I lay in my [bed] at ten o'clock that night. ... I then fell asleep, and beheld in vision something infinitely sublime. In the distance I beheld a beautiful white city. Though it was far away, yet I seemed to realize that trees with luscious fruit, shrubbery with gorgeously tinted leaves, and flowers in perfect bloom abounded everywhere. The clear sky above seemed to reflect these beautiful shades of color. I then saw a great concourse of people approaching the city. Each one wore a white flowing robe and a white headdress. Instantly my attention seemed centered upon their leader, and though I could see only the profile of his features and his body, I recognized him at once as my Savior! The tint and radiance of his countenance were glorious to behold. There was a peace about him which seemed sublime⬜—it was divine!

"The city, I understood, was his. It was the City Eternal; and the people following him were to abide there in peace and eternal happiness.

"But who were they?

"As if the Savior read my thoughts, he answered by pointing to a semicircle that then appeared above them, and on which were written in gold the words:

"These Are They Who Have Overcome the World⬜—
Who Have Truly Been Born Again!"

~President David O. McKay *Cherished Experiences from the Writings of President David O. McKay, comp. Clare Middlemiss, rev ed (1976), 59-60 paragraphing altered.*

"No one can preside over this Church without first being in tune with the head of the Church, our Lord and Savior, Jesus Christ. He is our head. This is his Church. Without his divine guidance and constant inspiration, we cannot succeed. With his guidance, with his inspiration, we cannot fail. …

"… I know the reality of his existence, of his willingness to guide and direct all who serve him."

~President David O. McKay *April 1951*

Scripture:

"And now, after the many testimonies which have been given of him, this is the testimony, last of all, which we give of him: That he lives!

For we saw him, even on the right hand of God; and we heard the voice bearing record that he is the Only Begotten of the Father—"
~Doctrine and Covenants 76: 22-23

Testimony:

"Angels appeared and said simply, "Why seek ye the living among the dead? He is not here, but is risen." (Luke 24:3–6.) Nothing in history equals that dramatic announcement: "He is not here, but is risen."

The fact of our Lord's resurrection is based on the testimonies of many credible witnesses. The risen Lord appeared to several women, to the two disciples on the road to Emmaus, to Peter, to the Apostles; and "after that," as Paul reported, "he was seen of above five hundred brethren at once. … And last of all he was seen of [Paul] also." (1 Cor. 15:6, 8.) …

As one of His latter-day witnesses, I testify that He lives today. He is a resurrected Being. He is our Savior, our Lord, the very Son of God. I testify that He will come again as our glorified, resurrected Lord. That day is not far distant. To all who accept Him as Savior and Lord, His literal

resurrection means that life does not end at death, for He promised: "Because I live, ye shall live also." (John 14:19.)"
~ *President Ezra Taft Benson* *The Meaning of Easter, Ensign, April 1992*

Reader,

So, you got to the end of my book. I hope that you enjoyed it and that it was useful to you!

I would just like to thank you for giving me your valuable time. I am truly blessed to have such a fulfilling occupation, but I only have that job because of people like you; people kind enough to give my books a chance and to spend their hard-earned money buying them. For that I am eternally grateful.

If you would like to find out more about my other books, then please visit my website for full details. You can find them at:

www.questcheney.com

Also feel free to contact me on Facebook, Twitter, Goodreads, or email (all of the details are available on the website), as I would love to hear from you.

LEAVE ME A REVIEW

If you enjoyed this book and would like to help, then you could think about leaving a review on Amazon, Goodreads, or anywhere else that readers visit. The most important part of how well a book sells is how many positive reviews it has, so if you leave me one then you are directly helping me to continue on my journey as a writer.

THANK YOU!

Thanks in advance to everyone who does this. It means a lot. I appreciate all of you who read my books and especially those who review them.

SIGN UP FOR MORE

If you would like more information about my books, or would like to be notified when my new books are being released,

SIGN UP ON MY WEBSITE

www.questcheney.com

About the Author

Jeff Cheney has worked as a civilian contract mechanic for the US Army, a heavy equipment mechanic, a High School teacher, and currently works in high technology computer chip manufacturing. He has been writing science fiction and fantasy stories for enjoyment for over thirty-five years and has published five SF novels with his brothers, as well as two QuEST books of Quotes.

He enjoys coaching youth basketball, working on cars and doing woodworking when the time allows. He has three grown children and lives in a small town in NW Oregon with his wife of 32 years.

Jeff has served in a multitude of callings in the Church of Jesus Christ of Latter-day Saints over the years; as a missionary in Guayaquil, Ecuador as a young man, and many others as the years have gone by.

www.ingramcontent.com/pod-product-compliance
Lightning Source LLC
Chambersburg PA
CBHW071842020426
42331CB00007B/1820